The Secret Gate

Serendipity Book One

Linda Field

HEDDON PUBLISHING

First edition published in 2022 by Heddon Publishing.

Copyright © Linda Field 2022, all rights reserved.

ISBN 978-1-913166-67-0

Cover design by Catherine Clarke

This is a work of fiction. Names, characters, businesses, places, events and incidents are either the products of the author's imagination or used in a fictitious manner. Any resemblance to actual persons, living or dead, or actual events is purely coincidental.

No part of this book may be reproduced or transmitted in any form or by any means, electronic or mechanical, including photocopying, recording or by any information storage and retrieval system, without written permission from the author.

www.heddonpublishing.com
www.facebook.com/heddonpublishing
@PublishHeddon

I would like to dedicate this book to my wonderful parents, Catherine and Philip Field, who sadly are no longer with us, but who taught me the importance of family life, supporting each other through all the trials and tribulations of life, and for always just being there.

About the Author

Linda Field is a nurse who has worked in the health service, higher education, and the private sector. She has always enjoyed creative writing, and has obtained a Diploma in Writing Prose and Fiction from the Regent Academy, London. She is an active member of the Balsall Common Writers group. (She is married with one daughter and lives on the outskirts of Coventry.)

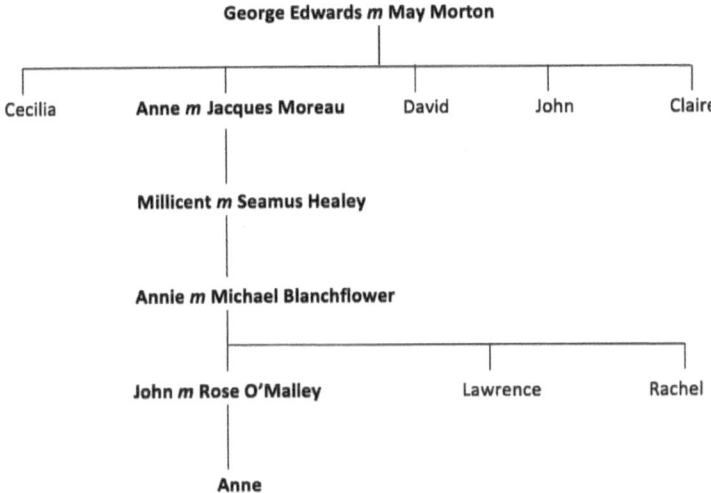

The Secret Gate

Chapter 1

George Edwards looked out of the breakfast room window. He was proud of what he saw. A large garden divided into 'rooms' comprising a rose garden, a cottage-type garden, a vegetable garden, and a small herb garden. Further on was the relatively large orchard, with apple, pear and plum trees, and this led to a bricked wall, which separated the garden from the open fields beyond. The garden complimented the newly built large, imposing house. George had accumulated wealth over the years from his family accountancy business, which he ran from the nearby town of Solihull, and he had decided to invest some of the money in the new property. He wanted to provide his family with a property that reflected his status in Edwardian society. His two sons, John and David, were away at boarding school, and his three daughters, Cecilia, Anne and Claire, were all being educated at home by their mother, May. They also had lessons in music, singing, embroidery, elocution, and other such accomplishments expected of young ladies in 1913.

Cecilia was seventeen, and quite the young lady. She had all the necessary attributes that should ensure she married well.

George's second daughter, Anne, was completely different. Although her father recognised that she played the piano, flute and harpsichord very well, he was frustrated by her stubborn disposition, and the fact that she showed no interest in finding a beau. At fifteen, she seemed to be frequently arguing with her mother. She had even tried to disagree with George, but was soon put in her place.

Nine-year-old Claire was different again. She had a sweet nature, which went with her angelic voice. She could frequently be found singing with Anne's piano accompaniment. Both would perform regularly at the evening soirees held at the family home.

Reflecting on his family as he finished his breakfast, George began to turn his mind to work. He had a busy day ahead, with quite a lot of appointments. He was not complaining, though, as appointments meant clients, and clients led to money in his pocket. Joseph the groom had the horse and carriage ready, and would take George off to work, and pick him up later at his request.

As the sound of the horse's hooves clattered on the cobbled stones, Anne knew her father was off to work. He left at 8.30am, every morning except for Saturday and Sunday. He would return about 5.30pm, and then the family would have evening dinner at 7pm. Everything was as regular and as predictable as clockwork in the Edwards household, beginning with breakfast at 7.30am, followed by lunch at 1pm, then tea at 3pm, the evening meal at 7pm, and a warm drink at 9pm, before bed.

Although Anne appreciated that routine was necessary, in her opinion it needed to be interspersed with other activities. She loved to escape with her music, and loved her piano, flute and harpsichord lessons with Mr Frazer. He had told her on several occasions that she was an accomplished musician, and should develop her talents further. He had also conveyed this sentiment to Anne's mother, but it had fallen on deaf ears. May believed that the primary aim of a girl's life was to marry well and play second fiddle to her husband for the rest of her life. Anne felt that May had been indoctrinated by George, with whom she would never argue or disagree. Anne vowed to herself that she would never be like that with any man.

That evening at dinner, George monopolised the conversation as usual, with Cecilia and May nodding and commenting at the appropriate time, and Anne trying not to listen. However, one topic of conversation did attract her attention.

'Those stupid Suffragette women are at it again. Would you believe that today one of them decided to throw herself under the King's horse at the races?'

No one spoke until eventually Anne said, 'That's terrible. To think she had to go to such extremes to get noticed!'

'Terrible? It's damned madness!' her father answered loudly. 'Don't you dare tell me you have any pity for these foolish women?!' He almost roared this last statement.

'Of course she doesn't!' May interjected.

'I do, actually,' said Anne defiantly.

Her father roared at her, 'Go to your room immediately!' Anne glared at him, and then at her mother. Cecilia and Claire sat with their heads bent down; not getting involved, as usual. Anne stood up, throwing her table napkin on top of her dinner plate, and marched out of the room. Ascending the stairs two at a time, she reached the sanctuary of her room, where she threw herself on the bed and cried tears of anger and frustration. Eventually, the tears subsided, and Anne dried her eyes. She lay on the bed, her eyes focusing on the patterned floral wallpaper adorned with paintings of several small birds ranging from robins to goldfinches. Anne so wished that she was a bird, and then she could fly away from this prison that was her home. She did love her bedroom, though. It felt like the only room where she could be her true self. The oak wardrobe and dressing table complemented the duck-egg-blue bedspread and dressing chair, giving the room a tranquil air. Her musical instruments were arranged in one corner, and her beloved books atop a small bookcase positioned near to the window.

She heard a light tap on the door.

'Who is it?' Anne asked tentatively.

'It's me, Claire.'

Anne jumped off her bed and opened the door to let in her younger sister.

'Come in,' said Anne. 'Are you okay?'

'Yes, I just wanted to check you were alright,' said Claire.

'I'm fine,' said Anne, hugging her sister. 'You'd better get off to your own room, before you are in trouble as well as me.'

'Alright. But I will see you later, for cocoa,' said Claire, a look of relief on her face. Anne closed the door after her. She was feeling quite hungry so decided to chance a visit to the kitchen, to try and find some food. Creeping downstairs, she noticed that her father had left his newspaper on the chair in the hall. She could not help noticing the headline, which read:

Woman throws herself under the King's horse at the Derby.

Picking up the paper, Anne read a bit more. **Suffragette Emily Wilding Davison threw herself under the King's horse, Anmer, as it rounded Tattenham Corner. She was killed instantly, and the Suffragettes now have their first martyr.**

Anne decided to read the article in more detail, so returned to her room with all thoughts of hunger dispelled. She read quickly, as she knew her father would be looking for the paper.

A few minutes later, she could hear him shouting, 'Where the hell is my newspaper gone? I left it on the chair.'

His annoyance made Anne smile, so she decided to keep hold of the newspaper, and let her father rant and rave about its whereabouts. Eventually, he returned to the study, where Anne knew he would soon fall asleep, and then she could return the missing newspaper. This she duly did, twenty minutes later. She crept quietly down the stairs, only to meet the housekeeper, Mrs Villet, at the bottom. Mrs Villet noticed the newspaper in Anne's hand.

'So it was you who has moved the newspaper,' she said, in her stern Scottish accent.

'I wanted to read a bit more about the Suffragette's death at the Derby races,' said Anne.

Mrs Villet tried to glare at her, feeling that she should, but a slight smile came over her face.

'I was really in search of some food, and was distracted by the headline on the paper,' Anne confessed.

'Well alright, just put the paper back. We do have some cold ham left from dinner, if you would like that with some bread?'

'Yes please,' said Anne, and she followed Mrs Villet into the kitchen.

Later that evening, Anne joined Cecilia, Claire and May for the mandatory hot cocoa. Her mother was very cool with her, so the sipping of the cocoa was a quiet affair, as no one spoke except to bid each other goodnight. As Cecilia and Claire left the room, May said, 'Anne, can I speak with you?'

'Yes,' said Anne. She knew what was coming. She prepared herself for a reprimand from her mother.

'I wish you would keep your views to yourself,' said May. 'Your father works hard all day, and wants some peace when he gets home. He doesn't want to hear about you sympathising with those Suffragette women.'

'Well, it was terrible what happened,' said Anne, hoping for some shred of agreement from her mother, but none was forthcoming.

'It was utter madness. Now get yourself off to bed, and forget about those silly suffragettes. As your father says, they all need locking up!' Anne scowled at her mother for the second time that day, then made her way back to her room.

That night, Anne slept restlessly, her dreams filled with visions of Emily Wilding Davison falling in front of the King's horse. The next day, she was fit for nothing, but had to endure a geography lesson with her mother in the morning. Luckily, the afternoon was better as she had a piano lesson with Mr Frazer.

Chapter 2

The remainder of the week was quite uneventful. Anne had been set some work to do by Mr Frazer, so was busy concentrating on this. She was studying the work of Handel, researching the life and work of this famous composer. She loved his compositions, and wished that she could compose such wonderful sounds herself. She was playing a piece by Handel when she was interrupted by her mother.

'Anne, don't forget you have a Latin lesson in half an hour.'

Anne had forgotten, having become so absorbed in her music. She hated Latin just as much as she loved music.

'Okay, I will be in the study soon,' was Anne's disinterested reply.

She sat through her Latin lesson under sufferance. The only thought which helped to facilitate the passage of the lesson was that she had the afternoon free. It was a glorious early summer's day, so Anne decided she would visit the garden and enjoy listening to the merry birdsong.

After lunch, Cecilia and May were going into town, while Claire played in her room. Anne made her escape out into the garden, ambled into the orchard, and perched on a bench. She admired the flowering buds on the apple and pear trees, and looked forward to when she could bite into the ripe fruit later in the summer. Dwelling on the thought of eating a tasty apple, she wandered down towards the brick wall, which surrounded the garden on three sides. Something drew her towards a small gap in the tangled hedge that covered the wall. As she spread the foliage apart, she found a wooden gate with a large rusty latch, which she promptly tried to push downwards. To her surprise, after a couple of tries, the latch moved, and she was able to push the gate open. She had to use some force to push it halfway, but this was enough for her slim body to pass through.

Anne was greeted by a magnificent view of rolling green fields, divided by trees and hedgerows. They looked just like a patchwork quilt of various shades of green and pale yellow. The clear blue sky complimented the blanket of green, and Anne was captivated by the cacophony of bird sounds. Suddenly, she felt free, and began to run across the field, the grass reaching her knees in places. She loved the feel of the blades of grass against her ankles, the remainder of her legs covered by her flowing skirt. As she stopped to catch her breath, she noticed a small figure in the distance, clad in a bright red colour, and standing out boldly against the green background. Anne wondered who it was, and she began to walk swiftly towards them. As she got closer, she could make out the figure was female, and carrying a rather large, flat brown case. However, as Anne got closer, the girl in red disappeared out of view, behind some trees. Feeling disappointed, Anne tried to see where the girl had gone. She waited a few minutes, but to no avail. The girl in red had disappeared as quickly as she had appeared.

Anne glanced up to the sky, as if hoping for some divine intervention, but none was forthcoming. Anne decided she should return home before someone discovered she was missing from the garden, so she ran back towards the half-opened gate and passed through it, then closed it quietly. Ensuring the latch was well covered by the foliage, she sauntered nonchalantly towards the house, just in time to hear her name being called.

'Anne, Anne!' It was her mother calling. 'Can you come and join us? We have some things to show you from our visit to town.' Anne was not interested in what they had bought. May and Cecilia had been buying some dresses for the summer, and Anne already knew she would not like them. They would be plain and boring and in pale pastel colours, unlike the dress of the girl in red. As she joined them in the house, she felt a renewed sense of contentment at her secret escape, and was determined to find out who the girl in red could possibly be.

The next day was Friday, and this meant another free afternoon. Anne planned to revisit her newly found escape route, and see if she could see the girl in red again. However, her plans were dashed by a change in the weather. At lunchtime, the rain had begun to fall lightly, but by two o'clock it had become heavy, and venturing into the garden wasn't an option. Anne was disappointed, and decided to drown her sorrows by playing some Chopin on the piano. Claire, who was also at a loose end, joined her. Claire sang and Anne accompanied her, and the afternoon improved until May decided that they had been performing for far too long, and should go and do something more useful, like studying the topics for their lessons the following week.

Anne and Claire returned to their rooms, and both pretended to revise the English literature and history for next week, but instead Claire played with her dolls in her doll's house, and Anne tried to write a song about the mysterious girl in red. She managed to compose a verse, after many crossings-out and much re-writing. She concluded she really needed to see the girl in red again, to help focus her thoughts.

The family were visiting relatives at the weekend, as it was Aunt Eva's birthday. Anne liked Aunt Eva, who was her mother's older sister, as she had a bit of spirit – unlike May. Eva had never married, but lived in a comfortable town house in Bath, with a collection of birds; including a parrot, who frequently spoke to everyone, much to their amusement.

Anne hoped the weather would improve for following week. The rain had persisted over the weekend, but they were still able to visit some of the shops in Bath, and dine in a superb restaurant to celebrate Aunt Eva's birthday. She was known at this particular restaurant, so they had made a cake which was adorned with candles, and everyone sang Happy Birthday. Aunt Eva was in her element. Anne and Claire were asked to perform, and everyone had an enjoyable evening.

The following week consisted of lessons with her mother, and two of the afternoons she had a piano lesson and music recital with Mr Frazer, which she enjoyed. She didn't have any free time to further explore her new escape route until the Thursday afternoon. However, by then, the weather had improved, and the sun was shining once again. Anne raced to the bottom of the garden and out through the gate, like a caged animal being released into the wild. It was wonderful to see the open fields once more. She made her way through the long grass, all the time looking for the girl in red, alas, to no avail. Eventually, she reached a shaded area, where she stumbled upon a babbling brook. The dappled sunlight reflected on the running water, which looked almost jewel-like, and dreamy. Anne settled on a stone close to the brook, and breathed in the sultry air. She began to feel sleepy, and decided to lie down on the soft grass beside the water. The birds were chirping, and Anne felt like she was in heaven.

'Hello.'

Dimly, Anne became aware of a voice. Coming to, she found herself gazing into the smiling, heart-shaped face of a girl with deep brown eyes and lightly tanned skin. The girl was pretty and young; probably a similar age to herself. She wore a bright lemon-yellow dress, which looked cool and comfortable. A wide-rimmed straw hat was tied loosely around her neck with a bright orange ribbon and nestled down her back, between her shoulder blades. She had a bag over her shoulder.

'Oh, hello.' Anne suddenly felt embarrassed in front of this stranger. 'I must have fallen asleep.'

'I know,' said the girl. 'I hope you don't mind. but I have been sketching you whilst you were sleeping.' She showed the drawing to Anne, who was amazed by the likeness.

'No, not at all. The drawing is really good. You are very talented,' said Anne, admiring the sketch.

'Do you think so? I'm sure I haven't got your nose and chin quite right.'

'It looks really good to me.'

'By the way, you will have to tell me your name. So, I can write it on the drawing.'

'My name is Anne. And what do I call you?'

'My name is Claudine.' The girl scribbled Anne's name on the drawing, then gave it to her. 'You can have this for being such a good model.'

'Thank you,' said Anne, taking the drawing from Claudine's outstretched hand.

'I have been hoping to meet you since I saw you the other day,' said Claudine. Anne was amazed, as she was about to say exactly the same thing. She told Claudine this.

'Great minds think alike,' said Claudine, smiling broadly at her newfound friend. Anne noticed the whiteness of her teeth, and thought they emphasised her beauty. She wished her own teeth looked that white. The girls began to chat, and discovered that they were neighbours, although their houses were some distance apart. Claudine told Anne that her mother was French, and her father owned a few perfumery shops, one being in Solihull and a larger one in Birmingham. She said she had several samples of different perfumes in her room.

Anne was envious. She was seldom allowed to use perfume, as her father thought it was 'all in bad taste'. On hearing this, Claudine promised to bring Anne one of the samples next time they met.

Anne suddenly began to panic, realising that she had been away from the house for quite some time. Claudine asked what was wrong. Anne made up an excuse that she was having a music lesson, not wanting her new friend to know the truth. They parted, promising to meet up again the next day. Anne knew she had the afternoon free, so she left Claudine, who was settling down to do another sketch.

'Before I go, I must ask you what you were carrying the other day. It looked heavy.'

'Yes, it is. That was my artist's easel, which doubles up as a large flat case, in which I can carry paints and a selection of brushes.'

'Do you use watercolour paints?' Anne asked, wanting to impress with her knowledge of art.

'When I am outdoors, I use watercolours, but in my studio indoors I often try to dabble with oils,' said Claudine. 'You must come and see my studio one day, if you like.'

'That would be fun,' said Anne, as she bid her new friend goodbye. She walked slowly to start with, but once out of Claudine's view, she began to run towards the secret gate, and was soon safely back within the confines of the garden. Thankfully, no-one had been looking for her. She ascended the stairs two at a time, and glided into her room, flopping down on the bed. She couldn't remember when she had had such a good time, and she reflected on the past hour or so spent with Claudine. It had been so relaxing and nice to be able to talk to someone of a similar age to herself. Although they seemed to come from different backgrounds, they did appear to have quite a lot in common. She had already detected that Claudine had more freedom than she did. Perhaps it was because her mother was French, or perhaps her father was not a tyrant like George.

The evening passed as uneventfully as usual, and as Anne got into bed that night, she looked forward greatly to seeing Claudine the following afternoon.

Chapter 3

The next day was glorious. Anne endured her elocution lesson in the morning, her mind on her secret rendezvous in the afternoon.

'Anne, I do wish you would concentrate, and stop daydreaming.' Her mother interrupted her thoughts.

'Sorry.' Anne decided to pay attention; the lesson would end sooner that way.

After lunch, there was a familiar tap on Anne's bedroom door. Cecilia. *What does she want?* Anne thought, but she said, 'Come in.'

Her sister promptly entered the bedroom, and sat down on the chair by the window. 'Mother has asked me to speak to you.'

'Has she?' Anne replied, dreading what was coming next. Had her secret escape been discovered before it had really begun? 'What about?'

'It's an invitation we have received from an eminent family, Lord and Lady DeCourtney, who live just outside Solihull.' Anne was still confused as to what it had to do with her, but breathed a sigh of relief to know her secret was safe. 'Mother wants you to play the piano for them when we visit for afternoon tea this Sunday next.'

'That's fine,' said Anne, 'but why couldn't Mother ask me herself?'

'It is to be a very important visit, as I am possibly to be matched with their son, so I'm to advise you on what music to play.'

Well, you're no expert on music, thought Anne. 'So, what will you have me play, then?'

'I thought something quite regal, like an aria by Mozart or Beethoven.'

Anne almost laughed. *Since when has Mozart or Beethoven performed an aria?* Her sister didn't have a clue.

'I'll think of something appropriate, don't you worry,' said Anne nonchalantly.

'But I do worry; this is very important to me, so I don't want anything to go wrong,' said Cecilia anxiously.

Anne began to feel quite sorry for her. 'I will play a piece for you before we go, so then you can tell me if you are happy with it. I will do my best to play well, and I promise I won't let you down.'

Cecilia gave her a rare hug, and left the room with shoulders drooping. Anne was grateful that it was not her who was being paired off with a suitable beau. She would have to tell Claudine all about it.

One hour later, Anne and Claudine were chatting amicably. They were sitting in the middle of an open field, taking in the view. Claudine had set up with her easel and, using her watercolours, was trying to capture the view on paper. Anne learnt that it was Claudine's ambition to be a famous artist, just like Renoir or Constable.

'How do your parents feel about your ambitions?' Anne asked tentatively.

'They don't mind. They appreciate I do have a talent, and they encourage me to develop it.'

'Your parents must be quite liberal, to allow you to think about working as an artist even though you are a female,' said Anne, reflecting on her own parents' views.

'That's a load of pebbledash!' admonished Claudine.

Anne was surprised by this reply and wanted to explore it further. 'What do you mean?'

'All this nonsense about women staying at home and having children is becoming outdated,' Claudine explained. 'Why shouldn't women have careers too?'

'I agree,' Anne interjected. 'So, I presume you are a supporter of the Suffragette movement?'

'Definitely!' said Claudine, nodding her head as if to add further endorsement to this statement. 'What do you think of my painting so far?'

Anne surveyed her friend's work and decided it looked superb. Somehow, Claudine had managed to perfectly capture the afternoon sunlight on the open fields, and the shadows cast by the wispy clouds in the sky.

'It's really good. What does your mother think of the Suffragettes?' Anne asked as Claudine continued with her painting.

'She supports them too, although she didn't agree with that woman throwing herself in front of the King's horse at Epsom the other day.'

'I know – wasn't that terrible?'

'What she hoped to achieve, I'm not sure. I think it has only helped to support the negative view of Suffragettes, that they are all mad – and this won't help the movement.'

Anne thought about this for a moment and then said, 'Yes, but she did it out of sheer desperation – just to get noticed, and this she did achieve, as it was the main headline in my father's paper.'

They continued their rhetoric about the Suffragettes, and then Anne told Claudine about her forthcoming performance for Lord and Lady DeCourtney on Sunday. Claudine had heard of the DeCourtneys, as her father had recently sold them some exclusive perfume.

'I believe they are very rich, so you had better mind your manners,' Claudine teased Anne.

'I'm more concerned for my sister, who is trying to make a good impression on them so she can become betrothed to their son.'

'Well, I wish her the best of luck. You must let me know how it goes,' said Claudine as Anne prepared to leave. 'I will have to bring my brother Jacques to meet you next time. He is also a musician, so you will have a lot in common.'

'I didn't know you had a brother.'

'You never asked, and before you ask me anymore, he is two years older than me, and attends a music college in London. He will be home next week, so we will have to suffer him playing the piano and sometimes the clarinet all day long, for several weeks over the summer.'

Anne was intrigued, and really wished to know more about this brother, but she had to go. As she headed back towards her house, she felt another wave of excitement at the thought of meeting Jacques. She wondered whether he would have the same dark looks as Claudine, in which case he was bound to be handsome – and he was an accomplished musician as well! Her mind full of Claudine and her brother, she made her way through the secret gate. Strolling between the fruit trees in the orchard, something made her look up towards to house, and for a moment she could have sworn she saw the upstairs curtains move. She dismissed it, thinking her mind was playing tricks on her.

As she entered the house, she could hear Mrs Villet discussing with the maid the eminent arrival of John and David, her twin brothers. They would be making an appearance the next morning, and would be home from boarding school for the summer break. There would be no more peace in the house, Anne concluded. Both her brothers, particularly David, had the same male arrogance as her father towards her and her sisters. They believed their role was to belittle females as much as they could. Anne sighed as she went upstairs to her room.

Chapter 4

Saturday was busy with the arrival of John and David, and the usual large amount of fuss being made of them, mainly by May. The boys were their usual boisterous selves, and began teasing both Anne and Claire over lunch. Cecilia hadn't joined them, as she was feeling a little under the weather. Anne knew the real reason was that she was suffering with a bad bout of "nerves", as a result of the arranged afternoon tea at the DeCourtneys the following day. Eventually, Cecilia did appear for evening meal, but she looked pale and drawn. Her mother asked her to stay behind after the meal. Anne couldn't help loitering outside the dining room door and eavesdropping on the conversation between May, George and poor Cecilia. It was all centred around how Cecilia should behave at the forthcoming visit.

Poor thing – she will be a nervous wreck by the time tomorrow comes. She felt a hefty tap on her shoulder, which made her squeal with surprise. Turning around, she came face-to-face with her brother David.

'You shouldn't be listening!' he said piously. By this time, her mother had opened the dining room door, and demanded to know what was going on.

'Anne was listening at the door,' said David, a smug look on his face. May glared at Anne, and then her father got involved.

'How dare you listen in on conversations that have nothing to do with you!' George yelled at Anne.

'Nosey parker, squash tomato!' David called, grinning.

Anne went to head upstairs to her room, but her father caught hold of her arm, shouting, 'Where do you think you're going? I haven't said you can leave.'

She could hear the anger in his voice as he snarled at her, his face red with anger. It made her shake with fear as to what might happen next. Meanwhile, Cecilia and May went into the drawing room as if nothing had happened. George was squeezing her arm quite firmly now, and she tried to wrench herself free.

Glaring at her, he did eventually let go, and stormed off to join May and Cecilia. Anne felt humiliated. David had watched the whole scene. Her arm was quite painful, so she began to rub it.

'Does it hurt – shall I rub it better for you?' said her brother, sarcastically.

'No thanks!' was Anne's reply as she quickly mounted the stairs to her room. She so wished that she was meeting Claudine the next day, instead of visiting those damn DeCourtneys.

The following morning came with more beautiful weather. Anne longed to make her escape through the secret gate, but instead she was helping Cecilia with her attire for the grand visit to the DeCourtneys. Cecilia was so nervous, she couldn't even decide what to wear. Eventually, she decided on a pale blue blouse with a navy skirt. Her long golden hair (her best feature, in Anne's opinion) was curled up neatly in a bun, and her make-up was minimal, consisting of a pale pink lipstick and a slight powder rouge to her face. Anne had advised this, since her sister looked so pale otherwise. Finally, Cecilia was inspected by both May and George, and eventually it was time to go. The party consisted of May, George, Cecilia and Anne, who all clambered into the waiting carriage. The boys and Claire remained at home, watched over by Mrs Villet. Anne so wished she was staying behind with them.

Most of the journey was in silence, and it seemed an eternity until they arrived at the DeCourtneys', where their carriage was greeted by two footmen, who helped them descend. The house was on a grand scale, with a very large entrance hall. *There must be at least a hundred rooms*, Anne guessed as they entered. Their coats and shawls were promptly removed, and taken away by an elderly man, presumably the butler. They were then led into the drawing room, which was adorned with several plush seats covered in a peach damask, which complimented the large cream rug.

The butler said, 'Lord and Lady DeCourtney will join you very soon. I will see to the refreshments.' With that, he left the room.

All the Edwards family were in awe of the grandiose surroundings. They perched gingerly on the edge of their chairs, in a state of trepidation.

This is going to be an interesting afternoon, Anne thought as she gazed at the grand piano in the corner of the large room.

All present became aware of the sound of a bell ringing, and then the elderly butler tottered in and formally announced Lord and Lady DeCourtney. The couple swept graciously into the room and headed for two individual chairs situated close to the large fireplace. As she seated herself comfortably, Lady DeCourtney greeted her guests with a smile. *She looks lovely,* Anne thought as she studied Lady DeCourtney's dress. It was pale pink and made of silk, embellished with a floral brocade lace around the collar. A small floral decoration contrasted beautifully with her chestnut hair, which was swept up in a loose bun. Her complexion was that of a typical English rose; pale, with a slight rosy tint to the cheeks, and soft pink lips.

Her husband seemed to fade into insignificance next to his wife, but he spoke with authority. 'Lady DeCourtney and I would like to welcome you to our home, and hope you will enjoy your afternoon tea.' He rang the bell and two maids entered, carrying curates laden with tiny, sweet wafers, small cassava cakes, hot bouillon with bread sticks and buttered rolls, hot muffins, cress, some fanciful, sweet sandwiches, and a dish of bon bons. The curates were placed on small tea-tables, positioned close to where each of the Edwards were seated.

'Thank you. If you could bring the tea in now,' said Lady DeCourtney. The maids both curtseyed before leaving the room, and returned with trays holding china tea pots with several cups and saucers. Seeing all this, Anne thought she had landed in heaven. She glanced over at Cecilia, who looked pale and nervous.

As the tea was served, they all had to introduce themselves, and Lady DeCourtney told them to please call her Edith, and her husband's name was Crispin. Anne wanted to laugh when she heard this name, but instead placed a bit of hot muffin in her mouth. She noticed that Cecilia was not eating much.

The conversation flowed quite well, even if it was a bit stilted. George and Crispin spoke about the state of the economy, and Edith and May focused more on fashion and the weather. Anne and Cecilia were not really included in the conversation.

'Matthew will be joining us shortly,' said Edith. 'He has been out riding this morning. He loves nothing better than going for a ride each day, to uplift his spirits and improve his constitution.' At this statement, Cecilia dropped her cake on the floor, and began apologising profusely as the maid was called to clear up the mess and refresh the teapots. Cecilia was blushing all over by now, and Anne felt sorry for her. She noticed May looking embarrassed after this incident, even though it was made light of. A few minutes later, Matthew entered the room and strode confidently over to his mother.

'Ah, Matthew, do come and join us. Crispin, ring for some more tea for Matthew. You must be thirsty after your horse ride, my dear?'

'I'm not too bad, Mother.' Matthew glanced surreptitiously at the guests as his mother introduced everyone, leaving Cecilia to last, as if to emphasise her presence. The conversation continued as Matthew was serviced with a plate, and a cup of tea. Anne noticed he didn't take milk with his tea.

It was mainly Edith and Anne who kept the conversation going. Anne was asked about her music, which she was happy to discuss.

'We look forward to hearing you play later,' Matthew interjected quite unexpectedly. Anne found herself smiling at him. She subtly studied his features. He hadn't inherited the beauty of his mother, but looked more like his father. He had a rather small face, with a pointed jaw and a long nose. His hair was curly and dark brown, and his clothes were equally as dark as his hair. His best feature, Anne decided, was his green eyes, which seemed to sparkle like cats' eyes. He was relatively tall and thin, but Anne noticed he had a hearty appetite as he tucked into the cake and sandwiches.

Cecilia suddenly began coughing profusely. It seemed that her tea had gone down the wrong way. May instructed Cecilia to stand up, and she began patting her on the back. Cecilia seemed to be getter redder and redder in the face, so the maid was called, and water was summoned. Eventually, a very embarrassed Cecilia was breathing normally again.

After the incident, it was decided that Anne should play for them. From the piano, she cast a quick glance at Cecilia, who still looked terrified. Anne began to play, and soon Matthew was standing behind her, humming the tune she was playing. She suggested that he join her in song. He became slightly flustered at this suggestion, saying, 'Oh no, I couldn't possibly join in – I would most certainly spoil your performance.' This response made Anne smile. She continued to play happily, performing some further requests from Edith.

'Do you play any instruments?' Edith asked Cecilia.

'N-no, I do not,' Cecilia replied quietly.

'Oh,' said Edith. 'Then what talents do you have?'

Cecilia didn't reply; she seemed to be gulping for air, so May interjected. 'She is very good at embroidery, and has an excellent head for arithmetic and Latin.'

'I see. Matthew, perhaps you would like to show Cecilia our newly designed rose garden?' Edith suggested, glancing at her son.

'Yes, Mother – what an excellent idea.' Matthew stood up and offered Cecilia his hand. She responded quickly, and the two of them left the room. Anne had finished playing, so sat quietly while Edith and May continued to chat mundanely. George and Crispin had excused themselves, and had gone off somewhere together. Anne was beginning to feel bored, and wondered when the visit would end.

Soon after, Cecilia and Matthew appeared in the hallway. They seemed to be chatting amicably. They entered the drawing room, and resumed their original seats.

'Well, Cecilia, what do you think of our rose garden?' Edith asked.

'It is beautiful, and the scent from the roses is intoxicating,' said Cecilia, sounding the most relaxed she had been all afternoon.

'Yes, it is – very captivating,' said Edith, looking pleased with Cecilia's reply. Crispin and George then returned, and the latter suggested that they should take their leave. He thanked both Edith and Crispin for the wonderful afternoon tea. Very soon, the butler appeared with their coats and shawls, and the carriage was summoned, and before long they were climbing into the carriage and travelling down the drive towards the main road. They all seemed to breathe a sigh of relief, glad that the experience was over. Anne would have to quiz Cecilia later, about how things had gone with Matthew.

Chapter 5

The next day was sunny and warm, and Anne looked forward to making the great escape through the secret gate that afternoon. Her brothers had gone off horse-riding, and Cecilia was chatting to May in the drawing room. Anne hadn't yet had a chance to ask Cecilia about yesterday's visit to the DeCourtneys, or how she had got along with Matthew. She was certain that was probably the subject of Cecilia and May's discussion. Half-tempted to eavesdrop, but wary after the incident the other day, she loitered outside the drawing-room door. She became aware of a voice behind her.

'Anne, would you play for me so I can sing, please?' Claire asked, looking pleadingly at Anne. She had nothing planned for the moment, so was quite happy to accompany Claire, and the two of them retired into the music room. They spent a happy hour singing and playing in unison, and eventually were joined by May and Cecilia. Claire's throat was becoming quite hoarse from all the singing, so May asked Mrs Villet to organise some cold drinks for them all, to have in the garden. They chatted amicably, and Anne suggested to Cecilia that they should have a walk around the orchard.

'Well, how were things with Matthew yesterday?' asked Anne tentatively once they were out of earshot.

'Alright – I suppose.'

'That doesn't sound very positive,' said Anne as they sat down on a garden bench.

'Mother and Father didn't feel it went very well.'

'Why? I thought it did,' said Anne. She had an urge to place a comforting arm over Cecilia's shoulder, but felt inhibited to do so. Her relationship with her older sister always felt quite stilted. They had never been very close, although Anne was feeling an increasing fondness for her older sister.

'They said I was very nervous, and didn't come across well.'

'Oh, ignore them – how did you get on with Matthew when you went out into the rose garden?'

'Fine – he is nice, and quite easy to talk to.'

'Well, there you go – that's what's important. So, what happens next?'

'I'm not sure. I think we have to wait for further correspondence with the DeCourtneys. They probably think that I'm not suitable for their son.' Cecilia looked quite dejected.

'Why ever not?!'

'Well, I don't play any instruments. I can't sing–'

'Yes, but you have other talents,' Anne interjected.

'Like what?'

'You have excellent needlecraft skills, and you excel in Latin.'

'Mrs DeCourtney didn't seem to be very impressed with these skills.'

'It's not up to Mrs DeCourtney,' said Anne.

'But it is.' With this, Cecilia stood up and headed back to where May and Claire were sitting. Anne followed her, and reflected on how unfair this notion of family matchmaking was. She vowed that she would never become a victim to it, even if it meant that she would never marry.

It was soon time for lunch, and the return of the twins, who quickly put an end to the peace as they raced around the hall like wild cats. May eventually had to tell them to sit down, and to please be quiet. Over lunch, they began to boast, particularly David, about their experiences at boarding school. Anne began to switch off from the idle chatter, focusing her thoughts on her great escape later that afternoon.

After lunch, everyone dispersed and went to their respective bedrooms. Anne was full of anticipation for meeting up with Claudine. Perhaps her brother would be there, too. Anne had decided to make her escape sooner rather than later. Making her way down the stairs, she passed David.

'Where are you escaping to?' His question spooked Anne a little.

'I'm off to enjoy the garden in this good weather.'

David leaned forward so that his face was about five inches away from hers and said, 'You're not having a secret meeting with anyone in the garden, are you?'

Anne was gobsmacked, and just stared back at David, not even proffering a reply. She continued marching quickly down the stairs, and eventually was out in the garden, heading towards the orchard. Still, she felt quite unnerved after the conversation with her brother.

He can't possibly know anything about my meetings with Claudine, Anne thought as she arrived at the secret gate. Making her way through it, she glanced back towards the house and, like before, she thought she saw the curtains move in one of the upstairs windows. It spooked her. Could it be David, spying on her? She scolded herself for being so nervous, and once in the open fields she began walking quickly towards the collection of trees that cleverly hid the babbling brook. The weather was very warm, and Anne wished that she had put on her straw hat, to protect her face and head from the sun.

As she entered the shaded tree area, she could hear muffled voices. Drawn towards them, Anne made her way towards the water and there she espied Claudine and a young gentleman, who Anne deduced must be her friend's brother. She began to feel nervous as she approached them. They were deep in conversation, and had not heard her arrive.

'Hello,' said Anne quietly. There was no reply. 'Hello,' Anne tried again, this time a bit louder.

Claudine turned around. 'Oh Anne, it's good to see you, I have been telling Jacques all about you.' The young gentleman, clad in a white open-neck shirt and dark trousers, turned around, and Anne found herself gazing into the deepest brown, dreamy eyes.

'Hello – good to meet you.' Jacques offered Anne his hand.

Placing her hand in his, she noted it felt soft and warm. Anne studied his face more closely. It was similar in shape to Claudine's, but the jaw was more masculine. His hair was also a dark brown, and quite curly.

His mouth was curved into a large smile, and his teeth were set perfectly between the fleshy lips. Anne became conscious that she was staring, and felt lost for words.

'Nice to meet you too,' she said eventually. She noticed that Claudine had been busy, with her easel and paint pallet in place, so she focused on her friend's painting.

'That looks good,' she said, and Jacques agreed.

'Yes, it is good. My sister is very talented.'

'Would you like some lemonade?' Claudine asked Anne, who gratefully accepted the glass being offered to her. The three of them were seated on the grassy bank, close to the water's edge. Claudine decided to take off her shoes and paddle in the cool water. Before long, Anne and Jacques joined her. The water felt so refreshing on their warm feet. Soon, they were merrily splashing each other. Anne couldn't remember when she had experienced such fun. Eventually, they settled down on the grassy bank once more, and Claudine resumed her painting. 'Anne, tell Jacques about your music,' she suggested. As Claudine concentrated on her painting, Jacques and Anne embarked on a discussion on different types of music. Anne found out that Jacques played the piano, and also the clarinet. He was studying music, and was hoping to play professionally in an orchestra, and travel. It seemed they both shared a love of music by Chopin and Handel but differed on their appreciation of Beethoven and Mozart. Jacques informed Anne that he had performed many solo performances, both publicly and within his family, and Anne said she had done the same. She told him about her desire to become a professional musician just like him, but knew this was impossible due to her parents' attitudes regarding the role of females in Edwardian society. Jacques told her that her parents had old-fashioned attitudes and needed to change.

Anne had lost complete track of time, but knew she had been gone for a long while. She had told Claudine and Jacques about the infamous trip to the DeCourtneys', and how Cecilia had been so nervous. They had both sympathised with poor Cecilia. Claudine asked about the suitor, Matthew. Anne gave a brief description of him, which seemed to make both Claudine and Jacques laugh.

Eventually, Anne decided that she had better take her leave. They arranged to meet the next afternoon at the same place, and Claudine and Jacques bade Anne goodbye.

'Nice to have met you,' said Jacques.

'You too,' said Anne, and she began to walk swiftly through the field, towards her house. As she neared the secret gate, she began to walk quicker. Once inside the confines of the garden, she ran towards the house. She didn't know what the time was, but knew she had been gone for some time. May was in the garden, pruning the roses.

'Hello Anne, I thought you were in your room. Where have you been hiding?'

'I have been sitting on the bench in the orchard, enjoying the lovely weather,' Anne lied, but her mother seemed to believe her.

'Yes, the weather is very clement at the moment, although I fear some rain tomorrow.'

Oh no, Anne thought – she didn't want the weather to prevent her from meeting up with her new friends.

That night before she went to bed, Anne thought about the lovely time she had spent with Claudine and Jacques. She was so glad she had met them, and hoped it would not rain the next day. As she dropped off to sleep, she pictured Jacques' handsome face, and imagined how wonderful it would be if they were both famous musicians, working together in the same orchestra, performing solos, and bowing to rapturous applause from the audience.

Chapter 6

It seemed Anne's mother had been right about the weather. It was raining the next day, and quite heavily, too. Anne hoped that it would improve by the afternoon so she would still be able to escape to meet her new friends. She decided to read her book after breakfast, but before long Claire was pestering her to play the piano so that she could sing. Anne didn't mind. The two were soon ensconced in the music room, and happily singing, but it was not to last. Their brothers, being bored, had other ideas.

They ran noisily into the music room, pretending to be planes flying frantically around the room, with David deliberately encircling the piano and making a loud droning noise, which succeeded in obliterating any tune Anne was playing.

'Go away, you two, and leave us alone,' Anne commanded, standing up from the piano in an attempt to assert some authority. Her plea fell on deaf ears. The boys continued with their activity. This time she yelled, 'For goodness' sake, go and play in your room, or anywhere else but here!'

David stopped in his tracks, and stood very closely face-to-face with Anne. Although he was younger than her, he was a good three inches taller. Looking down on his sister, David said, 'Make us stop!'

Anne glared back at him and said, 'You need to grow up – you're supposed to be thirteen years old, and yet you act like three-year-olds.' Anne could see Claire smiling, but David was not.

He seemed to be lost for words for once, but eventually said, 'Come on, John, let's go and find something more interesting to do.' And with that, David marched out of the room, John following after like a puppy trotting behind his master.

Anne felt rather pleased with herself after this encounter. She had successfully managed to deal with her obnoxious brother, and had won. Or so she thought.

The rain didn't ease up in the afternoon, so Anne had to content herself with other activities, realising that she would not be seeing Claudine or Jacques. Instead, she decided to try and write a song about them. After several attempts, Anne was quite pleased with what she had written. She tried to put the words into a song, but this wasn't quite so successful. Still, undeterred Anne carried on. About an hour later, there was a tap on the door. Reluctantly, Anne said, 'Who is it?'

'It's me, Claire.'

Anne smiled to herself. She enjoyed her younger sister's company, so didn't mind being disturbed. They had developed a camaraderie, which helped Anne through the difficult times with her father and mother. Anne always felt she could confide in Claire, knowing it would go no further. 'Come in,' she said.

Claire trotted in and sat on the chair near to the window. She gazed out at the rain, watching the water trickle down the windowpane.

'I heard you singing, so was wondering what the song was. I didn't recognise it.'

At this stage, Anne didn't want to share with Claire the content of the song, as she wanted her friends to remain anonymous.

'The song is not very well known. It's one which Mr Frazer has asked me to practise with, to see if I can change some of the tune.'

'Well, it sounded very nice to me,' said Claire.

Anne gave up any hope of furthering her song composition, and instead began to chat to Claire about different genres of music.

The afternoon passed slowly, and eventually it was time for the evening meal; an activity Anne did not look forward to. Her father commanded all the topics of conversation, as usual, but as the meal progressed, she was surprised when George said, 'I hear you have been harassing David and John.' The statement was directed at Anne.

'I don't know what you mean. It's more like the other way round,' said Anne, somewhat surprised.

Her father continued to look at her disdainfully. 'Please explain,' he said. Anne went on to tell George about the boys' activities, and how they had interrupted her and Claire's performance, which was taking place, rightfully, in the music room. When she had finished, everyone seemed to be glaring at her. She could see a smirk appearing on David's face.

'That's not the story I heard,' said George. 'I believe the boys were in the music room, and you ushered them out so that you and Claire could perform.'

Anne could feel her hackles rising. She looked at Claire for some support, but Claire's eyes were cast downwards.

'Well, I'm telling the truth, so you can believe who you like!'

This response caused George to become angry, and he flew at Anne. 'Don't you dare speak to me in that flippant way! Go to your room immediately!'

Anne stood up and walked slowly out of the room. She felt like the whole family were against her. Even Claire was too frightened to speak out. Anne ran swiftly up the stairs. *I hate this place!* she thought as she slammed her bedroom door and threw herself onto the bed. *I must get away from here before I go mad.* She started to heave as the tears came, and she found herself physically shaking, out of rage and anger at the unjust situation she found herself in. She vowed she would never speak to her father or her brother David, ever again.

Anne had a very unsettled evening and night. She continued to ponder on the unfair way she had been treated. *The boys are always right.* She thought this several times over, but didn't know what to do about it. She felt helpless in her own home, and longed to be far away. She foolishly toyed with the idea of going to live with Claudine and Jacques. Surely they would understand her situation, and want to help. Feeling hungry and sad, Anne was unable to sleep, and eventually decided to go down to the kitchen, to see if she could find some food. Although she was carrying an oil lamp to light her way, the gas light in the hall illuminated the staircase, and she could see the grandfather clock in the hall said the time was quarter-past-two. She crept silently into the kitchen, and attempted to light the gas lamp, so she could see what she was doing. After a few attempts, she succeeded, and found some bread and butter to sate her appetite. She drank some milk, then decided to return to her room.

Extinguishing the light, she left the kitchen and made her way to the hall, only to be met by Cecilia, who had clearly been crying.

'Cecilia, what's the matter?' Anne enquired in whispers.

Cecilia was clearly surprised to see her. 'I can't sleep.'

'Me neither.'

The two girls ventured into the kitchen, where once again Anne lit the gas light – more adeptly this time. They warmed some milk, and began to chat.

'So, what's preventing you from sleeping?' Anne asked.

'I was worrying about the other day, and our disastrous visit to the DeCourtneys. We haven't heard anything, so that's not a good sign.'

'Perhaps you are not meant to marry him. There will be others,' said Anne reassuringly.

Cecilia smiled. 'I can't afford to be too choosy. I'm no oil painting, and I have few talents.'

'You're always underestimating yourself,' said Anne.

'Well, it's true.'

'It's only true if you believe it to be true.'

Clearly uncomfortable, Cecilia changed the subject. 'Let's talk about you, and the carry-on at dinner last night.'

Anne did not really want to talk about this. 'There's not a lot to talk about. Father obviously believed David and John's version of the events, as always,' said Anne, shrugging her shoulders in a defeatist way.

'You always seem to rile Father. You know he does not like us to argue with him, so it's better to just keep quiet.'

'Well, that's where you and I differ,' said Anne. 'Why should we always keep quiet? Women have been treated as the underdogs for far too long – it's time things changed.'

'You sound just like one of those Suffragettes!' said Cecilia, laughing.

'Yes, well perhaps when I'm older, I will become one, and let's see what Father will think of that!'

'He will never let you,' said Cecilia.

'He can't stop me when I'm older,' said Anne, defiantly.

'Oh, but he can. He could decide to sever any allowance you might have, if you don't marry who he decides is suitable for you.'

'Well, let him!' said Anne, who felt a new determination rising in her.

'It's late. We had better get back to bed,' said Cecilia eventually, and she extinguished the gas light. The two girls trudged up the stairs to bed, bidding each other good night.

As Anne entered her room and got into bed, she knew what she had to do – try and attend one of those Suffragette meetings. With this thought in her mind, she fell into a fitful sleep.

Consequently, Anne felt quite tired at breakfast, and both she and Cecilia were yawning at the table. George detected this. 'I think you girls have not got enough to do, and it's making you tired and slovenly. Mother, we shall have to find some work for them to do – perhaps in the garden?'

'Yes, dear. The weather looks better today, they can both help me to prune the roses.' Anne and Cecilia looked at each other.

I don't want to prune the damn roses, thought Anne. She just wanted to meet with her friends.

This she eventually did, but several hours later. As she passed through the secret gate, closing it tightly behind her, she breathed in the fresh air, before marching swiftly towards the secluded brook. It was warm and sunny, and she could see the outline of two figures in the distance, beyond the wooded area where they had met previously. As she got closer, she could see it was Claudine and Jacques, who seemed to be dancing amongst the wild grasses. She began to run towards them, but caught her shoe in the hem of her long skirt, and fell face-down into the long grass. By the time she had recovered, Jacques had reached her, and was kindly helping her to her feet. Feeling embarrassed, she quickly got up, and found her left ankle was hurting slightly.

'Are you okay?' he asked, as Claudine arrived on the scene.

'I'm fine,' said Anne.

'Are you sure? One minute you were there, and the next you had disappeared into the grass,' said Claudine. Anne hobbled towards Claudine, and she put out her arms to embrace her friend.

'Oh dear, you seem to be limping.' Claudine was concerned.

'Really, I'm fine – it just hurts a little, but it will go off.'

'Jacques, do the honourable thing, and carry Anne down to the brook.' Jacques willingly did no other than sweep Anne off her feet, and began to run quite quickly with her. Anne yelped with surprise, but couldn't help laughing as Jacques was moving with her in his arms.

If Father could only see me now! she thought mischievously. Jacques placed her carefully onto the ground as they reached the edge of the brook.

'Thank you,' said Anne, gazing up into Jacques' kind face. Once again, she was drawn by those deep brown eyes and his wide, friendly smile.

'My pleasure. Are you sure you are alright, after your fall?' he asked. By this time, Claudine had arrived, and Anne began to quiz them about the dancing. Claudine informed her that Jacques was to go to a summer ball being organised by the music college he attended in London.

'He doesn't have a clue about dancing, so I was trying to teach him how to waltz. Can you dance, Anne?'

'Not really,' said Anne.

'I bet you can dance better than Jacques!' Claudine suggested. 'Why don't you two have a go?'

Jacques and Anne looked nervously at each other, but, coaxed by Claudine, Jacques eventually offered Anne his hand, and slowly but surely, Anne's injury all but forgotten, they were waltzing around by the side of the brook, her ankle making a miraculous recovery. The weather was warm, but there was a gentle breeze cooling them as they moved around. As they grew more confident, Jacques began to swing Anne around a little faster, until she became quite breathless, but felt completely exhilarated. Finally, through exhaustion, they stopped dancing, and collapsed onto the ground.

'How's your ankle?' Jacques enquired, and all three burst out laughing.

'Fully recovered, it would seem!' said Anne.

Claudine and Jacques remembered they had to go, as they were eating early that evening. Anne also realised it was getting late.

'Until tomorrow,' said Jacques and Claudine in unison, and Anne thought she saw Jacques wink at her. Becoming conscious that she had been missing from home for some time, she raced back towards the secret gate, and headed into the house. She was met by David, who deliberately stood in her way, so she had to go around him. For once, she didn't say anything. She was feeling so happy after her adventures with Claudine and Jacques, and filled with immense anticipation for what their next meeting might bring.

Chapter 7

Unfortunately, Anne's hopes of meeting up with her friends the following afternoon were dashed, as her mother had other ideas. May had decided to take Anne and Cecilia shopping for some clothes for the autumn. Anne didn't even want to think of autumn; she was enjoying the summer weather too much, and wasn't relishing the outing. *Perhaps I can meet them this morning.* After she finished her breakfast, she decided to venture out.

'You seem to spend a lot of time in the garden these days,' May commented.

'I love being out in the fresh air. It's going to be another warm day, and it is a shame to be inside.' Anne prepared to leave, but May suggested that perhaps Cecilia could join her, as she was looking quite pale, and some sunshine would do her good. This was not what Anne wanted to hear. Luckily, Cecilia declined the invitation, saying she had planned to read a book.

Eventually, Anne made her way across the garden, and was soon through the gate, and walking briskly across the field. She could see a solitary figure in the distance. As she got closer, she could see it was Claudine, standing out from the greenery, in that bright red dress that she had worn the first time Anne had seen her. Although it was only a few weeks ago, Anne felt like she had known Claudine a lot longer. Claudine must have spotted her too, as she began to wave and run towards her. The two girls embraced.

'You're not usually out here in the morning,' said Claudine, slightly breathless after her run.

Anne explained about her unwanted trip to town with her mother and sister. Claudine told her about a forthcoming Suffragette meeting she was thinking of going to, and asked if Anne would like to accompany her. Anne was thrilled by this invitation, but she pondered how she would be able to escape from the house to attend the meeting. She decided to confide in Claudine.

'Oh, we'll think of something,' said Claudine, reassuringly. 'What about a music lesson?'

'Mr Frazer always comes to the house to give me lessons, and anyway he doesn't give lessons over the summer holidays,' Anne replied despondently. Claudine began to smile, and suggested that Anne could do a recital at her house, and go to the meeting from there. Anne was plagued with fear and doubt. 'How will you invite me when my parents don't even know I have met you?'

Claudine looked surprised at this revelation. 'You mean that your parents don't know about you meeting Jacques and me out here in the fields by the brook?'

'No, they know nothing about my secret meetings.' Anne suddenly felt both ashamed and embarrassed.

Claudine was astonished. 'Tell me more.'

Anne decided to tell Claudine about her father, and his strict approach towards her and her sisters. She told how he favoured her twin brothers, and was always picking on Anne because she had the audacity to try and answer back. She could feel tears pricking her eyes as she opened up to Claudine, who had placed a friendly hand on her arm. All Anne's frustrations seemed to be released as she told Claudine about some of the recent incidents. By the time she had finished, the two girls had walked to the babbling brook, and were seated at the edge, near to the water. Anne found the sound of the trickling water soothing.

'You poor thing,' said Claudine sympathetically. 'No wonder you want to escape.'

'I don't know what to do about it – I feel trapped.'

Claudine squeezed her hand and said, 'You must attend this Suffragette meeting – they may be able to help.'

'But how am I going to get there?' Anne asked in exasperation.

'I told you, we'll think of something.' said Claudine reassuringly. Anne became aware that time had moved on and, sighing, said, 'I had better head back before I am discovered. Thank you for listening. By the way, where's Jacques today?'

'He's gone to some musical event in London. He will be gone for a few days. Why, are you missing him?' Claudine asked in a teasing way. Anne felt herself blush as they made their way back towards their homes. Claudine seemed not to notice, instead asking, 'Will you be *escaping* tomorrow?'

'I hope so,' said Anne, as she bid goodbye to Claudine.

'Meanwhile, I'll think of some way of getting you to that meeting,' said Claudine, as she watched her friend run up to the wall and creep through the gate. She didn't know how poor Anne could live the way she did, and was grateful that her parents were far more liberal. As Anne entered through the secret gate back into the garden, she felt a great sense of relief at having shared her situation with another. She somehow knew that Claudine was going to be her salvation.

A few days later, there was an unexpected knock on the door. There were seldom any visitors to Anne's home, so everyone wondered who could be calling. Anne could hear her mother speaking to the visitor, and not long afterwards, Anne was summoned downstairs. She went into the drawing room, to be met by the familiar face of Claudine. Seated in the chair beside Claudine was a lady whose looks so closely resembled Claudine's, they could have been mistaken for twins. She assumed this must be Claudine's mother.

Anne detected her own mother was flustered, as she seemed to stutter as she spoke. 'These ladies are our neighbours, and they have come to request that you play for them next week at a soiree they are arranging,' said May, glancing at Anne.

'Oh, that will be nice,' said Anne.

'They appear to know Mr Frazer, who has recommended you.'

Mrs Villet entered, carrying a tray of tea and fruit cake. She placed it down on the table next to Claudine and her mother.

'Yes, Mr Frazer was singing your praises, and telling us what an accomplished musician you are.' It was Claudine who spoke. 'He told us you like to play Elgar, my mother's favourite, so we just had to have you play. The soiree is to celebrate mother's birthday, you see.'

'I do like to play Elgar, amongst others,' said Anne, as she sipped her tea.

'We should try and see more of each other, since we are neighbours,' suggested Maria, Claudine's mother. Anne could clearly detect her French accent, and thought it was wonderful to listen to.

Claudine, Anne and Maria chatted amicably over tea until it was time for them to take their leave. May remained quiet throughout. She seemed to be rather shy in front of Maria and Claudine.

Final arrangements were made, and goodbyes were said. Anne knew that Claudine had managed to manoeuvre the musical performance so she could attend the Suffragette meeting. She marvelled at her friend's abilities to get things done, and could not wait to catch up with Claudine later that afternoon.

The weather was warm and balmy as Anne ran quickly through the secret gate, out into the open fields, later that afternoon. She could see Claudine in the distance, and waved as she ran towards her. The two girls embraced, and began chatting about the earlier events. Eventually, they reached the brook, and seated themselves in their usual spot, under the shade of the trees.

'Your mother is really rather serious,' said Claudine.

'I know, I think she is really quite shy. She doesn't mix with anyone outside of the house.'

'That's a shame. It would do her good to get out more.' Claudine had her sketch pad with her, and began to draw some flowers that were growing on the bank. Anne wasn't sure what sort of flowers they were.

'Oh, they're foxgloves,' Claudine informed her. Anne thought Claudine knew a lot about all the different flowers and the names of all the trees. Anne hadn't really been taught much about horticulture, as her father felt that this was a topic more in keeping with males, although it was deemed acceptable for his daughters to simply prune the roses. She really enjoyed nature; watching the flowers grow, and the activity of the birds and other animals, fascinated her. She conveyed her thoughts to Claudine.

'I have a really good book on different species of birds, and other wildlife found in our countryside. You can borrow it if you like,' Claudine suggested.

'Thanks – that would be really interesting.'

The girls whiled away the next hour just chatting and enjoying the summer air, Claudine doing the occasional sketch. But before long it was time for Anne to return to her home, as it would soon be evening dinner. She told Claudine how regimented the mealtimes were in her house, and how everything was ruled by the clock. Claudine sympathised as she bid her friend goodbye. Venturing quickly through the gate, Anne was back in her prison once again.

As the week passed uneventfully, most days Anne managed to escape through the secret gate. She chatted with Claudine, and learnt all about what might happen at the forthcoming Suffragette meeting. The day before the said meeting was due to happen, Jacques had returned from London. He joined the girls, and was busy regaling them with stories of his experiences in London. Anne had been feeling quite nervous at the thought of seeing Jacques again, but didn't confide her feelings to Claudine. As he told his tale, Anne could feel herself blushing as he demonstrated a particular dance with her that he had watched others doing at the ball he attended.

'Why didn't you dance, then?' Claudine teased.

'I didn't wish to make a fool of myself, and anyway, I didn't have a partner.' As he said this, he smiled at Anne, making her blush yet again. As usual, their time together seemed to evaporate. Before she knew it, Anne was venturing back through the secret gate.

The next day was quieter than usual, as the boys had gone off to work with their father at his offices in town. Anne appreciated them not being around. She wanted to do some preparation before the Suffragette meeting that evening. She also decided that she should practise playing some tunes for her fictitious recital.

Eventually, the evening arrived, and Anne headed off, accompanied by her mother, to Claudine's house. It was a large house, similar in style to her own. It had an imposing front door, which was painted bright red. May commented on the gaudiness of this colour for a front door.

'I like it,' said Anne, defiantly.

'I thought you might!' May replied.

They rang the doorbell, and the door was soon opened by a middle-aged lady dressed in a smart navy-blue skirt and blouse. Anne assumed she must be the housekeeper. They quickly introduced themselves, and were invited in by the smart lady, who led them into the light and airy drawing room.

'I will let Mrs Moreau know you are here. I know she is expecting you.' With that, she seemed to flounce out of the room. Anne realised that she hadn't known Claudine's surname before. Maria and Claudine entered the room soon after, and both Anne and May were made to feel welcome. Anne noticed the nervousness in her mother again, as she went to leave quickly. This suited Anne, as she wanted her mother out of the way so that she could then go off to the elicit Suffragette meeting.

After May left, Anne was invited to have some tea with Maria and Claudine. As they chatted, Anne kept calling Maria Mrs Moreau, until she was told, 'Please call me Maria, Mrs Moreau makes me feel ancient.'

Claudine said that the meeting was due to start at 7.30pm, so they needed to leave shortly. Anne hadn't given any thought to how they were going to get there. However, she needn't have worried, as they were transported in the Moreau family's rather large carriage. Anne enjoyed the comfortable ride, which was far better than in her father's smaller carriage.

They arrived as a large number of people, mainly women, were gathering at the entrance to the hall where the meeting was to take place. Soon, everyone streamed in, and Anne, Maria and Claudine were glad they had come earlier and were able to get a seat. There was quite a crowd, with a lot of people standing at the back of the room. Anne was surprised how busy it was. On a raised area in front of the crowd were a table and several chairs. Anne assumed this was where the speakers would be sitting. There was a sense of excitement bubbling up amongst the crowd, just as the meeting was due to start.

As if by magic, the noise seemed to die down, and three smartly dressed ladies and one gentleman strolled onto the stage and sat in the vacant chairs. Anne became aware of the hush which had descended. You could almost hear a pin drop. And so Anne's first Suffragettes meeting began.

Chapter 8

The panel introduced themselves, then proceeded to outline briefly how the meeting would go. The lead speaker was a tall lady, who had a gracious air about her. She spoke clearly but softly, and seemed to draw the audience in with her dulcet tones. Her command of English was eloquent, and Anne could tell she came from a privileged background. Her cream blouse looked like it was made of silk, and it contrasted well with her light blue boucle woollen skirt. On her head she wore a flattened royal blue hat, which was adorned with some form of dried flowers and a blue velvet ribbon. Anne found this to be slightly distracting. She kept trying to recall the speaker's name, but then remembered that it was on the piece of paper they had been given when they entered the meeting. She glanced fleetingly at the paper and espied the name: ***Florence Judd accompanied by Jane Eden, Mary and Frederick Scott.***

As the meeting progressed, the rest of the panel spoke. The main theme of the talk was the current role of women, and why it needed to change. There were lots of cheers, and support from the audience as Florence spoke vehemently about how women were currently treated like second-class citizens, with no voice of their own. They were mere appendages of their husbands. Anne liked this description, and made a note to remember it for the future. The meeting lasted nearly two hours. Anne was surprised how quickly the time had gone. She had thoroughly enjoyed it, and found herself being swayed along by the enthusiasm of the crowd, who began to cheer and clap as the speakers' voices became more emotive.

At the end of the meeting, Anne, Claudine and Maria made their way to the exit door. It took quite a while to leave, as the crowd seemed to congregate just outside. There was information on the next meeting, and Anne picked up one of the leaflets.

'Do you want to come to the next meeting?' Maria asked.

'Yes, I think so. Do you?'

'Yes, I think I will,' Maria answered decisively. This sentiment was echoed by Claudine, and the three were soon climbing into the horse-drawn carriage, and were homeward bound. They all chatted about the meeting, the speakers, what they had said, and how determined they all were to change the current status of women.

'We need more women like them!' Claudine concluded.

As they neared home, Maria asked Anne if she would like to come in for some refreshments, but Anne decided she had better go home, as she had already been out for a number of hours, and didn't want to raise any suspicion. The Moreaus dropped Anne back near her own driveway, and, bidding Maria and Claudine good night, she walked up to her front door, which she tapped on lightly.

It was opened by Mrs Villet, who frowned at her before allowing her to enter. 'I think your mother was expecting you back sooner – it is after ten o'clock, and she has been quite worried.'

Anne felt quite annoyed by this statement, but knew she had better pop into the drawing room and speak to her mother. As she entered, she was surprised to find both her parents there. They seemed to glare at her simultaneously.

It was her father who spoke: 'Anne, you have been gone quite a while – it must have been a very long soiree!'

'Well, it was! Maria – I mean Mrs Moreau – kept asking me to play more tunes, and everyone was singing and really enjoying themselves.' Anne almost believed the lie herself.

Her father nodded. 'Well, get off to bed now, and let's hear no more about it.'

Anne was tempted to bow before she left the room. She felt like a scolded child, but couldn't help chuckling to herself as she ascended the stairs and reflected on what her father would say if he knew where she had really been.

As the summer progressed, Anne's visits through the secret gate occurred quite frequently, and she was able to see Claudine, and very often Jacques, on a regular basis. They would often discuss the Suffragette meetings, and Anne was quite surprised when Jacques seemed to agree with the sentiment conveyed by the speakers. She was not use to males being supportive of females, as this was never apparent in her household. She found herself becoming increasingly attracted to Claudine's brother. She liked the way he looked at her; it made her feel special somehow. She always looked forward to seeing him, and her heart seemed to skip a beat when she gazed into his deep brown eyes. Their love of music helped to seal the bond, and sometimes Claudine would feel a bit excluded when they were discussing musical notes, and the vagaries of the different composers.
    One day, Jacques suggested that Anne bring her flute, and he would bring his violin, and they could play a tune together. The thought of them playing together engendered both fear and delight for Anne as she returned to the house. She looked forward to the next day.

The weather was glorious as Anne made her way into the meadow at the bottom of the garden. She could see Jacques ahead. Carrying her flute, she ran to catch up with him. There was no sign of Claudine. Jacques informed her that Claudine wasn't feeling well, and would not be joining them. Anne felt slightly nervous at the prospect of being alone with Jacques. However, once they both began to play their instruments, she found herself relaxing, and enjoying the notion of playing outdoors. The rays from the sun were very hot, but they were both shaded by the trees surrounding the brook. Anne had never enjoyed herself so much – she didn't want it to end. They played several tunes together, ranging from Handel's water music, to Chopin and some Mozart, and they ended their performance with *Non lo dirò col labbro* from Handel's 1728 opera *Tolomeo*. The romantic undertones of this piece weren't wasted on them.

Eventually, feeling quite exhausted, Anne and Jacques sat down beside the water's edge, the implications of their final tune lingering in both their minds. Anne was aware of Jacques' closeness. He had brought a small flask of water, and offered some to Anne. She gratefully accepted. They chatted easily about different music compositions, and Jacques told Anne about the music college he attended. She envied him, and conveyed her feelings to Jacques, who said, 'There is nothing stopping you from attending, we do have some young ladies on the course.'

'Do you?' Anne was surprised.

'Admittedly, there are only two out of thirty of us – but it's a start.'

'I bet their musical abilities are of a very high standard,' Anne suggested.

'I would say just as good as yours.'

Anne felt herself blushing. She was aware the time was moving on, and she should soon return to her house. Eventually, with some reluctance, she made to leave. Jacques touched her hand gently to help her up, and Anne felt a tingle through her whole body. She became flustered, so gathered up her flute and musical papers, and began to walk towards the secret gate at the top of the meadow.

Jacques followed her. 'I have really enjoyed today. I hope we can do it again.'

'And me,' Anne shouted back as she began to run.

'Until tomorrow, then.' Jacques stopped following her, and watched her scramble quickly through the secret gate. He thought to himself, *What a fascinating young lady*.

On arriving in the orchard at the lower end of the garden, Anne's thoughts complimented Jacques'. *I really enjoyed his company today... he really has a way of making me feel special*.

The rest of the afternoon and evening, Anne seemed to glide around almost in a trance-like state. Even Mrs Villet noticed. and asked her if she was feeling quite well.

'Yes, very well thank you,' was Anne's reply. Over their evening meal, Anne remained silent, hardly listening to her father's idle chatter about his working day. Even her annoying brother David could not succeed in distracting her. Her thoughts were all focused on Jacques, and what the next day might bring. But alas, the next day the rain decided to come down heavily, so outdoor activities were out of the question.

Anne stayed in her room for most of the day, playing her flute. Later on, she migrated to the piano, and Claire joined her for a singing sojourn. Her twin brothers, who were also bored with the weather, decided to accompany their songs by howling loudly like strangled cats, until eventually Mrs Villet asked them to please keep quiet, as she had a headache. As the afternoon progressed, Anne tried to turn her attention to some needlework (not her favourite pastime), as she attempted to chat to Cecilia about her progress with Matthew DeCourtney. Cecilia informed her that there had been no developments on that front, and that was the end of the conversation.

'Don't give up so easily,' said Anne, trying to cheer Cecilia up.

'What do you expect me to do?' said Cecilia despondently. 'I can't get in touch with him myself, as that would be totally unacceptable.'

'Why not?'

'As I said – it's not the done thing. Mother and Father would never condone it.'

With that, a rather agitated Cecilia left the room. Anne felt quite annoyed to be left stranded with her needlework, which she had only taken up in order to chat to her sister. She pondered on the unfairness of Cecilia's situation. It was all down to being a female, once again.

The remainder of the day passed uneventfully, and Anne really hoped that the morning would bring good weather, and she could escape through the secret gate. However, the next day brought more rain, and Anne was confined to the house yet again. By the afternoon, the rain had subsided, and Anne prepared to venture out. Her mother observed her.

'Anne,' May called. 'Where are you going?'

'I'm just going out to get some fresh air.'

'You always seem to be going out, as you put it.'

Anne pretended not to hear this comment, and proceeded at full speed towards the kitchen, which led out into the garden. She walked very quickly towards the secret gate, feeling somewhat anxious following her mother's disapproval. At last, she made her escape, and began walking through the grass, which was still wet following the earlier shower. The hem of her skirt soon became damp as she headed for the canopied area where the brook was located. There was no sign of Claudine or Jacques. Feeling disappointed, Anne found herself at a bit of a loose end. She couldn't sit on the damp grass, so decided to continue walking across the meadow. She could see some cows grazing in the distance, and the rain had caused a slight mist to form over the fields. Anne began to feel her spirits rise as she took in the glorious view. She started to hum a tune, and began dancing in a waltz-like way. She was so wrapped up with this activity that she was unaware she was being watched by Jacques, who was hidden in the trees surrounding the brook. Eventually, he ventured out and strolled towards her, clapping his hands as he drew near. Anne stopped and looked with total embarrassment as Jacques stood beside her. He stopped clapping, and began to praise both her humming and dancing.

'I didn't know you were there,' said Anne, averting her eyes away from Jacques.

'I know, so you were uninhibited, and that made it even better!' Jacques tried to take Anne's hand, but her embarrassment increased, and she went to leave.

'Where are you going in such a hurry?' This time, Jacques managed to grab Anne's hand, and draw her towards him. Anne found herself inches away from Jacques' handsome face. Those dark brown eyes were mesmerising. 'Don't rush off so quickly – stay, and we can chat.'

Anne really wanted to stay, but the sensible part of her told her that she should leave. She decided to take notice of the latter, and, apologising to Jacques, she began to run back towards the house. She soon became aware that he was running after her and, being taller than her, his strides were longer, so he was able to catch up. In a somewhat breathless tone he said, 'Anne, why are you running away? I mean you no harm. Please, let us not part like this!'

Anne felt a bit ashamed after this comment and said, 'I'm sorry, Jacques, but I really have to get back to the house before my father gets home.'

'So, are we still friends, then?'

'Of course we are.'

Jacques kissed her hand gently, and bid her goodbye. Anne drifted back to the house in a mesmerised state. Handel's *Non lo dirò col labbro* was playing in her head.

She was quite oblivious to most of the discussions at the evening meal, and spent the remainder of the time thinking about Jacques. That night in bed, when she did eventually fall asleep, she dreamt about him. It was a nice dream, in which she and Jacques were playing Handel's tune, and going off somewhere together, and all was well with the world.

Chapter 9

Anne and Jacques' secret romance continued to blossom as they met regularly throughout that long, warm summer, but in time, Jacques had to return to the music college. They kept in touch by letter, these being passed on to Anne via Claudine. Anne had to ensure she secreted the letters away before her parents started asking questions. They managed to meet up when Jacques returned home, but this was more difficult in the winter, due to the unpredictable weather. Still, somehow, they found a way, and their feelings for each other developed into a loving and lasting relationship.

However, everything changed in 1914, with the outbreak of the Great War. Jacques was called up, and Anne was devastated by the fear of him being killed, and the thought of never seeing him again. She occupied her time, like so many others in her situation, by helping the war effort when she could. However, her father was against her joining any voluntary organisations, or working in any place where the work had previously been done by men. Her independent spirit found this very frustrating, as she longed to take on some of the roles associated with the men who were away fighting for their country. She still got together with Claudine when she could, and the two would console each other when they would hear about the many soldiers being killed. They continued to attend the Suffragette meetings, although these had fallen off somewhat during the war.

It was difficult for Anne and Jacques to maintain their long distance, secret relationship, but if Jacques was ever on leave, they had managed to snatch some brief but precious moments together, and these encounters only helped to make their love for each other deepen. And eventually, after many tedious years of fighting, the catastrophic Great War was over, and Jacques had managed to survive. He never spoke about his experiences of that terrible war, choosing to try and obliterate the gruesome memories from his mind.

Unfortunately, Anne's father had died; he had developed tuberculosis of the lungs, and subsequently died in 1918, as the war was ending. As the illness took hold of George, his personality seemed to soften, and he was less aggressive towards everyone, particularly Anne. Towards the end of his life, they would even have quite amicable chats, and George became more accepting of the changing role of women.

Following her husband's death, Anne's mother was totally grief-stricken, and Anne was landed with the task of taking care of the household, Cecilia, her brothers, and Claire. Cecilia had opted out of this role, being far too upset to cope with the responsibility. Anne was not enjoying the task one bit. However, free from the shackles of her domineering father, and with the indomitable support of her music teacher, Mr Frazer, Anne had obtained a scholarship to attend a music college in London. She was due to start in September 1919. She was so excited, as it was the same college Jacques had attended. He was proud of her when he found out her news.

Jacques was now employed as a clarinet player in a large national orchestra. Their relationship had moved on somewhat since those early youthful days, when she had escaped through the secret gate. Everything was now above board, with all the family members aware of their relationship.

May admitted that she had on more than one occasion spotted Anne returning through the secret gate, but had chosen to keep it from George, whose health at that time had started to fail. George's illness spanned a period of ten months, in which time he slowly deteriorated. Cecilia had also been aware of the existence of both Jacques and Claudine, but had said nothing. She had developed a jealousy towards Anne, and envied her sister's easy relationship with a handsome young man, while she continued to struggle to find a suitable partner. Nothing further had developed with Matthew DeCourtney, and Cecilia was convinced that he had actually been more interested in her younger sister, although she never voiced this insecurity to anyone. Before George died, he and May had continued to try and find a beau for their eldest daughter, but with no success. They had briefly tried the same approach with Anne, attempting to pair her up with Mr Frazer's son Edward, because he too played musical instruments, but Anne had her heart set on Jacques.

After the death of George, life at home had become far more congenial. The regimented lifestyle had slowly evaporated, and Anne was allowed to invite Jacques and Claudine to the house regularly. Both Anne and Claudine continued to attend the Suffragette meetings and even May, cajoled by Claudine's mother Maria, had attended one. By 1918, women had been given the right to vote, although the right for all women over twenty-one years of age was not granted until 1928, but positive strides forward had been taken. The contribution of women to the workforce during the war had strongly influenced this outcome.

Claire was blossoming into a beauty, who sang regularly at soirees, often accompanied by Anne on the piano. She was never short of suitors, and thoroughly enjoyed all the attention this afforded. David and John had achieved high grades in their studies, and were both away at university. David was going to take over his father's accountancy business, while John excelled in teaching. Anne still felt sorry for John, as he was very quiet and retiring, and always seemed to be in David's shadow, not able to make a decision without consulting his twin brother. David had remained precocious and arrogant, and was becoming more like his father George every day. Luckily, he only had to be tolerated at holiday times.

*

After completing her music course, Anne was lucky enough to join the same national orchestra as Jacques. This stroke of luck allowed them to see each other regularly as they toured around the country, and then on a European tour, playing in Austria, Germany and France. On reflection, this was one of the happiest times in Anne's life. Her mother's support for the Suffragette movement blossomed, in part thanks to her growing friendship with Maria. Claudine had fulfilled her ambition of becoming an artist, and was now living and working in Paris. Anne and Jacques hoped to visit her someday.

On 21st July 1923, Anne married Jacques, It was a grand day; the sun shone, and the wedding ceremony in the local church was superb. Hymns were accompanied by some of their musician friends, and the celebrations afterwards took place in the back garden of Anne's family home. The house had recently been named Serendipity, which was Anne's choice.

After the wedding, the couple were due to honeymoon in Europe, stopping off in Paris to visit Claudine. Those were memorable times, and Anne often reflected on them as the years passed, and she became a mother. Her daughter, Millicent Anne Moreau, was born on 1st April 1929. By this time, Jacques and Anne had stopped touring with the orchestra, and Jacques had taken up teaching music at the same college that he and Anne had previously attended. There were still some of the same teachers there who had taught them. Anne continued to play, and gave private lessons to students studying music. They lived in London, but frequently visited Serendipity.

May died, and Cecilia stayed living in the house with Claire, who was soon to be married. Cecilia still hadn't found Mr Right. She would tell Anne that she was not bothered, but Anne was not convinced. John also lived at the house, working as a teacher at a local grammar school, remaining quiet and aloof most of the time. He never quite recovered from the unexpected death of his twin brother. David had died suddenly, as a result of a serious horse-riding accident. He had sustained a severe head injury, and died instantaneously from a brain haemorrhage. David's favourite pastime had been riding his horse, and he had even taken to joining the local foxhunting clan, much to Anne's disapproval. However, she had rationalised it by believing that it fed her brother's aggressive and bullish streak, which had only worsened over the years. It was on a foxhunting expedition, whilst approaching a deep ditch, that David had been thrown from his horse high into the air, and he had landed head-first against a large boulder. His fiancée Constance had been devastated. The funeral was a quiet affair, with only family and a few friends attending. Although David had not been her favourite person, Anne was saddened by his untimely death, and felt great compassion towards Constance.

A few years later, Anne moved back to Serendipity, with her family. This was mainly to help support Cecilia and John, although both Anne and Jacques were also missing the countryside, and had tired of London, so the move was appreciated by all. Jacques managed to secure another job, teaching music at a nearby college.

Millicent grew up surrounded by music, so it was not surprising that she learnt to play the piano and flute, and had also developed a penchant for playing the violin. She was a clever, happy child, and Anne's only regret was her not having a little brother or sister to play with. She conveyed this sentiment to Jacques one evening as they sat in the garden at Serendipity.

'She seems quite happy to me. I'm not sure she would want to share with another,' he replied.

They watched Millicent as she played happily with Wisp, the family dog. Anne knew Jacques had a point. Millicent was now ten years old, and was not used to having to compete with a sibling. She attended the local school, as neither Anne nor Jacques wanted her to be tutored at home. Neither would they see her sent away to boarding school. School helped her to make friends, and there was always a constant flow of young girls and boys coming round to play.

Cecilia had remained unmarried, and still resided at Serendipity. She had offered to move out when Anne, Jacques and Millicent returned to the house, but they wouldn't hear of it. Cecilia and Millicent became great allies, spending many a happy hour shopping and chatting amicably to one another in the garden. Cecilia was a keen horticulturalist, and had taken on the role of chief gardener. She had transformed the garden beyond recognition, and had won an award for her garden from an esteemed local gardening society, of which she was a member. Anne was glad Cecilia had found her niche in life. Claire, on the other hand, had settled down, and married an army officer called Jack Millett. She now lived down south, and had two wonderful little girls, May and Anne. She spent her time taking care of them, and socialising with the other officers' wives and families.

*

After the devastation of the Second World War, Anne, Jacques, Millie, Cecilia and John all continued to live together at Serendipity. Things were tough for everyone as the country tried to put itself back together. There was rationing of many food items up to as late as 1954. This impacted the lives of all in the household. They no longer employed a housekeeper, but did have a cook and cleaner to help with the domestic duties. There was a lot of austerity in the post-war era, following the financial and emotional damage of the war. The country had been drained of resources. Anne was unable to give any private music lessons at this time, as money was a problem even amongst the middle classes. Life remained busy, with Jacques and John both out working, while Anne and Cecilia minded the house.

Millie had grown into a fine young lady. Academically, she had done very well, and had chosen to take up a career in law. Anne was a little disappointed she hadn't chosen music, as she could easily have followed in her parents' footsteps. But at the end of the day, the choice was hers, so she went off to London to study, and managed to gain employment as a solicitor following completion of her degree. She enjoyed the challenges her job afforded, and worked very hard.

Anne sometimes thought Millie spent too much time working, and not enough on socialising. Whenever she returned to Serendipity, she always looked drawn and tired. Anne found it difficult at times to get through to her, and sometimes felt she had little in common with her daughter. She envied the easy way Millie seemed to converse with Jacques, and even with Cecilia.

With Christmas approaching, everyone was preparing for the forthcoming festivities. It was one of Anne's favourite times of the year. As she trudged around the garden in the snow, she was drawn to the secret gate, even though she hadn't ventured through it for many years. She decided she would go through it.

The gate was very stiff to move, and creaked as it was opened. It reminded her of the first day she had gone through it, all those years ago. On reaching the other side of the gate, Anne marvelled at the magnificent view. The fields were covered with white blankets of snow, and the trees laden with glistening droplets. In the distance, she heard the squawk of a crow, and her eyes followed it as it soared through the clear blue sky. It was one of those crisp winter mornings when the air felt fresh, and even though it was icy-cold, her nose, fingers and toes felt warm. She sighed, and reflected on her life. It truly was serendipitous. She had found something good when she was not looking for it. When she had gone through that secret gate, she could never have expected to meet Claudine, or Jacques, or the many other opportunities which had opened themselves to her. That was why she had named the house Serendipity. The infamous Handel's tune *Non lo dirò col labbro* was playing in her head. The aria had since been adapted by Arthur Somervell in 1928, for voice and piano. Somervell's English language adaptation was aptly called *Silent Worship*. This version remained a popular classic in song recitals and home music-making and Anne had played it on many occasions, ensuring that Millie was able to play this memorable tune, too.

After several minutes of contemplation, Anne returned to the warmth of the house. John had lit a fire in the drawing room, which felt cosy and warm. Anne joined him and Cecilia as they decorated the Christmas tree. She could not believe that this Christmas would hail the end of 1952, and the start of another new year.

At midnight on New Year's Eve, the church bells were chiming out, inviting in 1953. Anne, Jacques, Millie, Cecilia and John began to sing *Auld Lang Syne* as they joined arms. There was a full moon, and Cecilia had been adamant that they step outside into the ice-cold night, to welcome in the New Year.

'I wonder what this year will bring?' Anne asked.

'Well, I hope it's a good one,' Jacques replied, as he grabbed both Anne's and Millie's cold hands and ushered them quickly inside. They celebrated with some malt whisky to warm up, only Millie declined, which Anne thought unusual. She mentioned this to Jacques as they prepared for bed later, but he seemed unconcerned. 'She was probably tired. It was late, after all.'

New Year's Day was spent languishing over a lunch of roasted pheasant, red wine, and sherry trifle, made by their wonderful cook Mrs Turner, who had cooked for royalty in a previous role. Feeling pleasantly satiated, Anne and Jacques decided to take a walk. Noticing that Millie was looking a little peaky, Anne suggested that she accompany them, but received a very staunch no. As they walked along in relaxed companionship, they reflected on the events of the previous year. Overall, it had been quite a good one. The country was slowly recovering from the effects of the war, and a lot of food was no longer being rationed.

Anne was still concerned about Millie, however. 'She looks rather pale, I hope she is okay.' She shared her concern with Jacques for the second time that day.

'I'm sure she's fine, everyone looks pale in the winter.'

Anne felt a little reassured by this comment. Eventually, they returned to the house, and decided to have an impromptu recital. Everyone cheered at the suggestion, and very soon Anne and Jacques were playing piano and flute, the others singing along to their favourite aria, *Silent Worship*. Even Millie reluctantly joined in.

Did you not hear My Lady
Go down the garden singing
Blackbird and thrush were silent
To hear the alleys ringing

Oh saw you not My Lady
Out in the garden there

> *Shaming the rose and lily*
> *For she is twice as fair.*
>
> *Though I am nothing to her*
> *Though she must rarely look at me*
> *And though I could never woo her*
> *I love her till I die.*
>
> *Surely you heard My Lady*
> *Go down the garden singing*
> *Silencing all the songbirds*
> *And setting the alleys ringing.*
>
> *But surely you see My Lady*
> *Out in the garden there*
> *Rivalling the glittering sunshine*
> *With a glory of golden hair.*

Anne could feel herself well up as she heard the tune, and now the accompanying words to the song. They always reminded her of when she and Jacques had first played the music together all those years ago. Jacques smiled at her, fully aware of why she had a tear in her eye. The rest of the day passed congenially, everyone feeling tired but contented, and retiring early to bed after their late night.

The holiday was finished far too soon, and everyone was preparing to return to work. Jacques had a busy term ahead of him, as did John. Anne was once more giving more lessons, and Cecilia had become more involved with the horticultural society.

Anne, still thinking Millie didn't seem herself, decided to discuss her concerns with her daughter one morning, the day before she was due to return to London. Millie was in her room, packing her suitcase.

'Millie, are you okay? You've been looking quite pale this holiday.'

'I'm fine,' Millie replied rather too quickly. She continued to cram her clothing into the suitcase.

'Well, if you're sure,' said Anne, detecting Millie's agitation.
'Yes, I'm sure.'
Realising she was getting nowhere fast, Anne decided to leave Millie, but still felt concerned. Something wasn't right.

Chapter 10

January and February passed rather slowly. The days were very cold and icy, and there were several downpours of snow, rendering journeys of any distance difficult. As a consequence, Anne gave very few music lessons. Cecilia was unable to do anything in the garden, and even Jacques and John were unable to go to work on a few of the days, when the snow had fallen heavily. They all looked forward to the spring, and the weather getting warmer.

Anne continued to venture through the secret gate, weather permitting, to admire the views beyond. She seemed to be visiting this place more frequently of late, and it seemed to be because Millie was so much on her mind. They had heard nothing from her since Christmas, which was not in itself unusual, as she was not the best of communicators. Anne sometimes wondered how her daughter was so successful at her job, which involved plenty of communication with clients. However, she consoled herself that Easter would soon arrive, preceded by Millie's birthday on 1st April. They always got together for this.

However, they received an unexpected letter from Millie, informing them that she wouldn't be visiting Serendipity for her birthday. She gave no real reason, other than pressure of work. Anne's suspicions were further aroused.

'This is most unusual,' she said to Jacques one morning over breakfast. Cecilia had breakfasted earlier and was outside in the garden, making the most of the finer weather which had eventually come around.

'What is?'

'Millie not coming home for her birthday.'

'We can't expect her to visit us for every single birthday forever. After all, she will soon be twenty-four years old,' Jacques reasoned as he bit into his hot toast.

'I know, I'm becoming like an old mother hen in my old age.'

'Old age, what old age?!'

'Well, I will be fifty-five next birthday.'

'That's not old, wait till you get to my age. I'll be sixty next year!'

'Gosh, where have the years gone?!' They ate the remainder of their breakfast in comfortable silence, and then Jacques went off to work. Anne had a piano lesson later that day, with a girl from the nearby village. Anne enjoyed the sessions with Alice, who had real potential to develop into a successful musician.

Anne sometimes unrealistically wanted all her pupils to have careers immersed in music. Often, such thoughts turned her mind to her daughter, and Millie's stubborn desire not to have a career in music. Anne wondered what she was doing, and decided to write to her.

My dearest Millie
How are things with you? We all missed you at Easter, and of course your birthday, did you get our card? I hope you are not working too hard – there's more to life than work, you know!
Everything is just the same here at Serendipity, your dad is busy working as usual, and I'm giving more lessons than ever. Cecilia continues to make the garden look superb, she truly has 'green fingers'. Well, I don't have any more news, so I will sign off. Look forward to hearing from you soon
All my love
Mum xxx

Anne posted the letter that afternoon. Somehow, she felt better after writing. Her afternoon lesson with Alice went very well too, and by the time Jacques returned from work, her spirits had improved.

Finally, May arrived, bringing with it some warmth, and a feeling of regrowth. May always reminded Anne of her mother, since she had been named after this month. It had been May's favourite time of the year, too; she had appreciated the changes that spring brought, and the effects on all the plants and trees. The trees were turning green, and the planted wheat seeds in the fields were starting to sprout. Anne felt she could even venture out without a coat. Jacques was fine as usual, Cecilia was happy coaxing her newly planted seeds to grow, and even John seemed quite cheery. Anne concluded that spring had a good effect on people. Her only concern was that she hadn't heard anything from Millie, even after sending the letter. She knew something was wrong; her maternal instincts told her so. She decided to pay her daughter an unexpected visit. In fact, Anne hadn't visited London for several months, and began to look forward to spending some time with her daughter, shopping, and perhaps visiting some of the local sights, too.

She discussed her idea with Jacques that evening. He was somewhat reticent in his reply: 'You know Millie might not appreciate a surprise visit, you might not like what you find.'

'What do you mean?' Anne was a little annoyed by this comment.

'Well, she might have a boyfriend there that we don't know about.'

'Don't be absurd, Millie doesn't have boyfriends!'

'Not that we know of. Remember, she is twenty-four, young, free and single in the capital!' Jacques winked as he said this last statement. Anne was not amused.

Despite her husband's warning, Anne decided to visit Millie as planned, and a couple of days later she found herself approaching Millie's flat with some trepidation. It was only 3 o'clock, so Anne presumed that Millie would be at work. She had a key, so let herself in. All was 'spick and span' inside, as expected. Millie had always been a very tidy child, and this was reflected in the fastidious tidiness of all the rooms. Anne liked the flat, and had been quite instrumental in helping Millie to rent it. The owner was an elderly man, who seemed to have a fatherly approach to renting his property. Some of the others had been very mercenary, asking for high monthly rentals.

The flat was quite small and compact, but the high ceilings gave it a feeling of spaciousness. There was a small kitchen, living room, and two bedrooms, a bathroom and WC. It was a sunny day, and the sunlight streamed through the windows, lighting up each room and reinforcing the feeling of light and airiness.

Anne ventured into the kitchen to make some tea. She noticed a crumpled piece of paper on the side, and couldn't help glancing at it. When studying the letter in more detail, Anne found it was a hospital appointment. Her fears had been justified. Millie was ill. But the contents of the letter were not what she had been expecting.

The appointment was at the ante-natal clinic, to see the midwife for a check-up. Suddenly, it all made sense. Millie looking pale, tired, and abstaining from alcohol – her daughter was pregnant, and she hadn't even known. But who was the father? Millie had never mentioned a boyfriend. Anne began to panic, hoping he was not married, which might explain Millie's secretiveness.

Anne was so absorbed in what she had found that she didn't hear the front door open. The next thing, Millie was standing right in front of her, a look of sheer horror on her face. Immediately, Anne noticed the unmistakable bump, emerging quite clearly from under Millie's tight-fitting black skirt.

'M-Millie, oh why didn't you tell us?' She was close to tears as she asked the question.

Millie didn't respond straight away, moving out of the confines of the small kitchen into the living room. She sat down, looking drained and tired. Anne sat opposite her and waited for her to speak.

'I didn't know how to tell you. I knew you would be disappointed, with me not being married. It has taken me quite some time to accept it myself.'

'I've got to ask you – who is the father?' Anne said quietly, as she gazed at Millie's saddened face.

'It is someone at work.' Millie was not giving much away, so Anne pressed her further.

'Who?'

'You don't know him.'

Of course I don't know him, I don't know anyone you work with!

Anne thought, exasperated at Millie's response.

'Why don't you ask me how I'm feeling?' said Millie, getting up and marching into the kitchen. 'Anyway, you haven't explained why you're here.'

'I thought I would surprise you.'

'Well, you certainly succeeded in doing that!'

'I'm sorry, I should have let you know I was coming, only I have been concerned about you since Christmas. I knew something was wrong.' Millie didn't reply so Anne continued, 'Can I ask when the baby is due?'

Millie started to boil the kettle to make some tea. 'It's due in late summer.'

'Is everything okay with it... the baby, I mean?'

'Yes, as you know, I am due to see the midwife on Monday.' Millie made the tea and carried the teapot and two cups on a tray into the lounge. 'How long are you planning on staying?'

'I haven't really given it much thought,' said Anne, sipping her tea. It tasted good. She hadn't realised how thirsty she was. 'I can stay as long as you want me to.'

'Really, there's no need, I am feeling fine now that that awful sickness has passed.'

Always so independent thought Anne, as she watched her daughter get up to visit the WC.

'I keep wanting to pee all the time now, though!' This comment made Anne smile, as she recalled the many ailments she had endured during her pregnancy with Millie. She felt a sudden gush of maternal protective instinct towards Millie as she watched her return.

'Would you like something to eat?' said Millie. 'Sorry, I have forgotten my manners.'

'Why don't we go out somewhere, my treat?' Anne suggested, realising that Millie probably didn't have a lot of food in the flat. 'You can relax, and not have to bother preparing any food.'

Millie agreed, and suggested a nice little restaurant a few streets away. Once inside, Anne had to agree the place had atmosphere and the food looked good, too. Millie began to relax a bit more and towards the end of the meal Anne decided to probe further as to the identity of the father. Still, Millie was giving nothing away. They returned to the flat and as they sat drinking their cocoa, Anne felt her eyes shutting, and Millie suggested that she went to bed.

Surprisingly, after the day's events, Anne slept well. The next morning, she could hear Millie busy in the kitchen. She decided to let her know she was awake, calling good morning to her daughter.

'Would you like tea in bed?' Millie called back.

'Oh, no thanks, I must get up – this is late for me.'

'You must have been tired.'

'Yes, I think I must have been,' said Anne as she appeared in the kitchen, stifling a yawn. 'I haven't been sleeping very well, I've been worrying about you.'

'So now you know the unexpected, you won't ever sleep well again!' said Millie as she buttered the toast. They ate their breakfast in the lounge, and planned how to spend the day. It was Saturday, so Millie wasn't working. After some discussion, they decided to visit Westminster Abbey, go past the Houses of Parliament and Buckingham Palace, and then finish with a shopping spree.

'You'll be tired after all this gadding about,' said Anne as they stopped to have morning coffee in a cafe overlooking the Thames. The day was warm and sunny. Anne was enjoying the time with Millie, despite the unexpected news. She still wanted to know who was responsible, and what he was going to do about it. She decided to try and find out that evening.

Several hours later, they arrived back at Millie's flat with tired, aching feet, and a few laden shopping bags. A cup of tea soon revived them, as they reflected on the day's activities. Anne had really enjoyed all the visits, and appreciated Millie's kindness as she offered to buy Anne a dress she had spotted in the window. Millie had insisted, telling her that it could be an early birthday present. Anne finally agreed, and as she modelled the dress back at the flat, she felt her relationship with Millie had gone up a few notches. She decided to tackle the burning question as to the paternity of the baby.

Millie gave a big sigh and said, 'The father is married.'

Oh no – my greatest fear! thought Anne, as she listened attentively to Millie.

'Like I said, I work with Sean – that's his name. I have known him a few years. He is married, but his wife suffers with depression and ... he began to confide in me about her. I foolishly began to feel sorry for him, and one thing led to another. It wasn't planned, and we both got carried away one night here in the flat – you see, he used to come here quite frequently, especially when his wife was really bad. She is in a mental institution at the moment, as her condition has become much worse.' Millie sighed and then continued, 'When Sean found out I was pregnant, he said he was going to leave his wife and take care of me and the baby. But I couldn't allow him to do that.'

'Why ever not?' Anne interrupted.

Millie stared at her, astounded. 'Mum, how could he leave his wife, who is already severely depressed? God knows what she might do – she has suicidal tendencies, you know!'

Anne hadn't thought of this.

Millie looked exhausted after her confession, and Anne suggested they both went to bed. Alone in her room, she had a restless sleep, and spent most of it trying to work out how things could be better for Millie and the baby – but no solutions were forthcoming.

Chapter 11

Millie decided to let Anne accompany her to see the midwife. The afternoon passed slowly, with Millie eventually seeing Mary, the friendly midwife, one hour later than scheduled, as she had to deal with an emergency on the labour ward beforehand. Mary was very reassuring, and told Millie and Anne that *Baby a*ppeared to be fine. She discussed the importance of eating a healthy diet, and having plenty of rest, and then another appointment was made for a few weeks' time. Anne found herself becoming emotional as the realisation kicked in that her only daughter was having a baby, and she would soon be a grandmother. She could feel an overwhelming need to protect and nurture Millie, and the baby growing inside her. Once the midwife had left them alone, Anne conveyed these feelings to Millie, wiping a tear from her eye as she spoke.

'I know this pregnancy has been a real shock for us both, but we must look to the future now; you and the health of your baby are the most important things. Your dad and I will give you all the support and help you need, we love you.' With that, Anne kissed Millie, and gently squeezed her hand.

'Thanks Mum, that's good to know,' Millie replied.

Anne thought she could detect watery eyes, as her daughter gave her a hug. This was a rare moment for mother and daughter, and Anne so hoped it would continue. Despite the somewhat unwelcome news, perhaps this would be the thing that brought them back together, as close as they had been when Millie was little.

The midwife had said, 'Try and bring your husband next time. We don't want the men to feel left out, do we?'

'I'm not married,' Millie had blurted out, much to Anne's chagrin – She thought 'Midwife Mary' didn't need to know this.

'Oh, I'm sorry, I just assumed a respectable young lady like yourself *would* be married,' Mary retorted, looking somewhat dismayed at this news. Anne could sense Millie's embarrassment.

'I'm afraid you're going to get a lot of that!' said Anne as they walked away from the hospital towards the bus stop. Millie didn't answer. She remained quiet for the rest of the journey, and that evening, too.

As they sat in the lounge after supper, Anne tentatively asked, 'I don't suppose I could meet this Sean before I go back home?'

Millie gave her a surprised look. 'Why do you want to meet him?'

'Well, I would like to meet the father of my first grandchild.'

Millie was taken aback by this reply and said, 'If you put it like that, I can't really refuse!'

She said she would try and arrange for Sean to pop round after work the following evening, and so the scene was set.

Anne was alone in the flat the next day. She didn't mind, as she needed some time alone, to collect her thoughts and take in all that had happened during this brief visit. As the afternoon progressed, she began to feel unexpectedly nervous, as she thought about meeting Sean. She wasn't sure how she would react to meeting this man who had effectively changed the course of her daughter's life.

Millie returned from work, and prepared a supper of cottage pie with green beans, followed by egg custard. Anne thoroughly enjoyed her meal and while Millie made the tea, she decided to change, before Sean arrived. He was due at 7 o'clock. There was a gentle tap on the door, just as the clock on the mantelpiece struck seven.

At least he's punctual, Anne thought as Millie opened the door. A tall, well-dressed gentleman entered. His hair was light blond, and slightly tussled across his forehead. He had soft blue eyes and freckled skin. He smiled and kissed Millie lightly on the cheek, then strode purposefully towards Anne, stretching out his hand.

'Hello Mrs Moreau, it's nice to meet you.' Anne took his hand. It felt warm and soft, and she thought she detected a slight Irish accent. She was thrown by his somewhat forthright manner. *Goes with the job!* she thought. *Dealing with all those clients.*

Millie went into the kitchen to make some tea. There was an uncomfortable silence as they waited for her to return.

'Millie tells me you play a lot of musical instruments,' said Sean, trying to make conversation.

'Yes, I do,' said Anne, 'do you play anything?'

'Y-yes, I can play the guitar badly, and can tap out a few tunes on the piano.'

Anne was suddenly impressed. 'Tell me more.'

Before Sean could respond, Millie had brought in the tea tray, saying, 'Oh yes, Sean can play quite a few tunes. His father played in an Irish Ceilidh band.'

'Did he?' Anne wanted to hear more about the musical connections.

'Well, since Millie has brought it up, I will tell you a bit more about my dad. He was actually born in Ireland, and he did play in a Ceilidh band, which toured all around the country when he was younger. My mother didn't enjoy him being away so much, so he gave it up and took up a respectable job in the Garda. However, he continued to play at local venues, but unfortunately he died last year, from a heart attack.'

'I'm sorry to hear that,' said Anne. 'What instrument did he play?'

'He played the guitar and the ukulele, and he would sing as well.'

After this revelation, Anne found she felt more relaxed in Sean's company, and the three of them settled into an easier conversation. They chatted amicably for a few hours, always skirting around the issue of the forthcoming baby. Eventually, Sean suggested that he had better head off home, as he and Millie had work the next day. As he got up to go, he said, 'It has been great to meet you, Mrs Moreau, and please rest assured I will give Millie all the support she needs during and after this pregnancy. I think the world of her, and if circumstances were different, I would marry her tomorrow.'

'I hope so,' said Anne, standing up to bid Sean goodbye. He

spontaneously reached over and kissed her cheek softly, and then followed Millie towards the front door. He bid Millie goodbye, whispering something into her ear before he went.

I hope it was something nice thought Anne, as Millie returned to the room with a big smile on her face. She was just like the cat that had got the cream.

The next morning, Anne was due to return to Serendipity. She was glad that she had discovered Millie's secret, even though the news was not really good. She wondered how Jacques and the others would react to the news of the forthcoming birth, and all that went with it. Travelling back on the train, Anne ran through the options for Millie following the birth. She could try and bring the baby up alone; she could insist that Sean marry her, and they would raise the child together (although this was probably not an option); she could have the baby adopted, and get on with her life... Anne was so deep in thought that she nearly missed her stop. She got off the train and Jacques was there to meet her. It was good to see him again, after the events of the last few days. She realised she felt quite emotionally drained. They embraced affectionately, and Jacques drove them home. She decided to tell him all the news once they were back.

They sat in the drawing room (they still called it this, although it should have been referred to as the lounge/front room), while Mrs Turner prepared the evening meal. Anne broached the subject of Millie and her recent visit; she didn't quite know how to break the news, so just came straight out with it.

'Millie is going to have a baby.'

Jacques looked at her in disbelief. 'What did you say?'

Anne repeated the sentence again. Jacques was clearly shocked.

'But how, when, and with whom...?' The words stammered out of his mouth. She told him everything, about meeting Sean, and the situation with his depressed wife, when the baby was due, the trip to the see the midwife, and how Millie was looking much better now she had gone past the morning sickness phase. It felt good to share the burden with another.

'It must have been quite a trip for you,' said Jacques, holding her hand. Anne agreed it had been.

A few weeks later, they decided to impart the news to Cecilia and John, one Sunday after lunch. They reacted very differently. Cecilia seemed quite nonplussed by the revelation, much to Anne's surprise. She seemed quite happy at the idea of becoming a great aunt, whereas John was rather damning.

'What a stupid thing to do!' was John's response. 'How does she intend to bring the child up on her own? She should have it adopted!'

Neither Anne nor Jacques knew how to react to this statement. Eventually, Jacques said, 'I'm sure Millie has thought a lot about what you have said, and realises that it won't be easy. The father has offered to support her as much as he can—'

'Oh, that is jolly good of him!' John interrupted. He seemed to be getting angrier. Jacques decided to drop the subject, as John was prone to having "anger fits" (as the doctor called them), often about the most trivial of things.

Psychologically, John seemed quite unstable at times. Anne felt some of this was due to him never having fully accepting David's death. He remained withdrawn a lot of the time, never socialising outside of his work. Unfortunately, recently he'd had an anger tantrum at work, and the doctor had prescribed a mild sedative to help calm his nerves. Anne was not convinced that tablets would help. So most of the time John was left to his own devices at Serendipity, either in his room or in the drawing room. He seldom seemed to venture out, even to the garden. Anne had hoped that he would perhaps meet someone who he might settle down with, although this seemed highly unlikely now, as he was getting on in years, and had not shown any inclination towards the fairer sex. She wondered if this was due to his shyness, or perhaps his sexual inclination.

She had read a little about homosexuals, and had mentioned her suspicions about John to Jacques, whose reaction was to laugh out loud.

'I think he's just very shy, and has had little opportunity to meet anyone.'

'But there have been female teachers at the school where he works,' reasoned Anne.

'Yes, I know, but he's got to speak to them, and get to know them.' Anne decided to abandon the topic of John's sexuality and instead concentrate on Millie, who was now almost eight months pregnant. She came for a visit and Anne was pleased to see that she was looking very well. She seemed to be happy. The baby was "kicking" regularly, and Millie concluded that she/he was going to possibly be a dancer! She told Anne that Sean had been very supportive, even insisting on attending her appointments with the midwife, despite some of the judgemental looks he received. Sean's wife Victoria wasn't improving; in fact, if anything, she seemed to be getting worse. The whole situation sometimes made Anne fear for the outcome, and what might happen after the baby was born.

The baby decided to arrive earlier than expected, and after a prolonged labour, Anne Elisha Moreau was born at 5.30am on 15th August 1953. She was a "perfect baby"; not crying too much, feeding well (Millie had decided to try and breastfeed, after encouragement from the midwife), and generally doing all the cooing and gurgling sounds that newborn babies do. Anne adored her, and was constantly offering to pick her up, help with bathing, or changing her nappy, which seemed frequently to be full!

After the birth, Millie had decided to stay at Serendipity for about a month, so the rest of the family could help, and Sean would try to visit as often as he could. All the members of the household doted on Annie, as she came to be called, so as not to confuse her with Grandma Anne.

Jacques was constantly admiring Annie, particularly at night-time, when she lay fast asleep in her cot. Cecilia and even John became involved in caring for the little one, and a true sense of harmony descended on Serendipity. Even though Millie felt constantly tired, she was coping very well with the new baby. Sean visited some weekends, and Anne observed his and Millie's close relationship as they both looked after their daughter. She wished things were different, and they could be married and have a proper family life. She secretly feared how little Annie would grow up and be accepted, coming from a single parent family. Although attitudes towards this situation were changing, there was still a lot of stigma and scorn cast by many in society.

After the mandatory month, Millie returned to London to care for Annie on her own. They had been surprisingly understanding at her workplace, leaving her job open until she felt able to return. Most employers would have more than likely terminated her employment, frowning on her condition as an unmarried mother. Millie was grateful, but wasn't sure when or how a return to work would be possible. However, she enjoyed her one-to-one time spent with Annie, who continued to thrive, and was growing into a pretty baby.

When Millie took Annie to the see the nurse, everyone commented on her adorable blue eyes, blonde wispy hair, and infectious smile. There were similar reactions when Millie pushed her in the pram around the park and to the local shops.

There were many visits in the coming months, from all family members, except John. They came to offer support to Millie, but most of all they came to see Annie. On one occasion, Anne and Jacques brought their musical instruments and played several tunes to the baby, who cooed, and happily clapped her hands.

'I think she's going to be a musician,' said Anne to Jacques one day, when they were alone in Millie's flat. They had just finished singing *Silent Worship* to Annie, and she seemed to sway happily to the tune, entranced when Anne and Jacques started to sing.

'Don't start on about her being a musician, especially in front of Millie,' said Jacques, pointing a finger at his wife in jest.

'I'm sorry, I can't help it. I would so love her to follow in our footsteps, but you're right, I'll try to keep my thoughts to myself.'

Chapter 12

In 1954, Millie eventually returned to work after a year of motherhood. She had employed a very pleasant Irish girl called Trisha to mind Annie while she was at work. Luckily, she was not expected to work full-time, so did mainly mornings or afternoons, having Monday or Friday as her day off. Annie continued to develop into a lovely little girl, and Sean visited frequently, so she recognised him as Daddy, even though he was not there all the time.

Events relating to Victoria went from bad to worse. Her depression became deeper, and she frequently suffered psychotic episodes, when she had to be hospitalised for her own and others' safety. After one such episode, she had tried to attack Sean with a breadknife, thinking he was plotting to kill her. Her medication was increased, but this didn't seem to help, and her psychiatrist had suggested ECT (electro convulsive therapy), as he had seen good results in some patients following this treatment. To Sean, the treatment seemed barbaric, but he was willing to try anything to help improve his wife's condition.

Her condition did temporarily improve after four ECT sessions, but sadly she reverted back to the psychotic episodes. Sean began to visit less, finding it painful to watch his wife deteriorate. On one occasion, Millie had gone with him, and was shocked by Victoria's appearance. She looked thin and gaunt, with dark, sunken eyes staring into space. She was not really aware of their presence. Not long after this visit, she began to develop suicidal thoughts, and the nurse found her trying to tie a ribbon tightly around her neck one evening.

Annie was nearly two, and was happy playing in the lounge of Millie's flat when Sean appeared unexpectedly at the front door.

'Dadda... Dadda...' Annie was calling as Sean entered the room. He looked distraught. Millie knew something awful had happened.

'She's dead. She managed to kill herself, I knew she would in the end.' Sean blurted this out as he collapsed into the chair.

'Oh, I'm sorry – how d-did she do it?'

'She managed to jump out of the window, and landed on the hard gravel path. She was still alive, so they rushed her to hospital, but she died a few hours later.' Annie got up and toddled very slowly but purposefully over to Sean. He gently caught hold of her hand, and pulled her towards him as he began to cry. She stroked his head, trying to comfort him. The whole scene brought tears to Millie's eyes.

As the year passed, the awful events of that fateful day slowly began to fade. Sean sold the house he had lived in with his wife, and moved in with Millie and Annie. They settled into harmonious domesticity, and began to plan to buy a house in London. One evening, Sean arrived home, smiling from ear to ear.

'What's made you so happy?' Millie enquired as they sat down to their evening meal.

'I think I've found us the perfect house.' He showed her the details, and on reading the specifications in more detail, Millie had to agree. The following day, they went to view the property, leaving Annie with Trisha. The same day, they put an offer in, which was accepted by the vendor. They just had to sort out the finances. That weekend, Sean asked Millie to marry him, and so the plans were made for an Easter wedding the following year. They spent the whole weekend celebrating. Not too long after, they managed to move into the house and get settled.

It was Easter 1956, and the weather was surprisingly warm as they all piled out of the small local church. The wedding, back home near Millie's parents', had been very low-key, with Millie looking very smart in a cream shift dress and matching slingback shoes, and Sean handsome in his dark blue suit, white shirt, and plum-coloured tie. Little Annie looked scrumptious, in her lemon dress and white lacy bonnet. As usual, she had a big smile on her face.

The small wedding party returned to Serendipity for the wedding meal. Mrs Turner had surpassed herself for this event. There was chilled melon for starters, followed by crown roast of lamb with potatoes and parsley butter, peas with mint cream and chestnut cream, and the dessert was vanilla ice-cream with tutti-frutti, and then small cakes with coffee to end the meal.

They sipped champagne to toast the happy couple. Everyone felt exceedingly full after the feast, and due to the clement weather, they were able to sit outside in the garden. As expected, Anne and Jacques had teamed up for the inevitable soiree of musical recitals, including *Silent Worship*. Millie informed Anne quite adamantly they weren't called soirees nowadays. Everyone gathered enjoyed the remainder of the day, and retired to bed shattered.

After the wedding, Sean and Millie went to romantic Paris for their honeymoon, leaving Annie with Anne and Jacques. Anne had asked them to look in on Claudine, if they had time; she was still living there and working as an artist, although Anne hadn't heard from her for some time, so was anxious to know that she was okay. Millie and Sean managed to locate Claudine's abode, but it was not good news. They managed to glean some information from a neighbour. Apparently, Claudine had been living with another French artist, and both of them had upped and left quite suddenly just a few weeks earlier. They had left no forwarding address. Anne was perturbed by this news, as she had maintained a constant correspondence with Claudine over the years. She conveyed her concerns to Jacques.

'You know what Claudine is like – she's so unpredictable,' said Jacques as they discussed Claudine over breakfast.

'I know, but she has always kept in touch. I don't know much about this artist friend of hers, except that he is French and called Jean. You know how besotted she can get with her men friends.'

Over the years, Claudine had had many men friends, but had never married, being the free spirit that she always professed to be. There had been no children – Claudine had categorically stressed that she was not the maternal kind. She spent her life painting, mainly still-life, and to supplement her income she gave some private tuition to up-and-coming artists. In fact, she had met many of her men friends this way, so consequently many of them were younger than her.

After some reassurance from Jacques, Anne decided to stop worrying about Claudine, and hoped that she would hear from her soon. In the meantime, she was enjoying looking after Annie whilst Millie and Sean were on honeymoon. She was regularly playing the piano with her, and Annie was attempting to sing along a lot of the time, much to Anne's and Jacques' amusement. Anne was convinced that her Annie would become a musician.

*

Anne's predictions were correct. Annie grew up to become a very accomplished musician, playing the piano, keyboards, acoustic guitar, clarinet, and ukulele. She also did well academically, and passed her eleven plus. She attended a grammar school in London, which was renowned for a musical bias.

By the time she was twelve, Annie had decided she wanted to choose a career in music, and so began working towards achieving her goal. All the family, especially Anne, were so proud of her, and attended all the performances she gave as part of the school's orchestra. She frequently performed solos, playing piano, clarinet and latterly the guitar. This was the instrument she enjoyed playing the most.

By the time she was eighteen, Annie had been accepted at the same musical college both her grandparents had attended years earlier. Jacques had stopped teaching there a long time ago, but his reputation went before him. Sometimes, Annie found it a little tiresome when her grandfather's status and many achievements were very often discussed with her and fellow pupils. Although she was very proud of her grandfather, she didn't want to hear about it all the time, although she would never let on about her feelings to Jacques himself.

Annie graduated three years later with a degree in music, and various accomplished high grades in piano, acoustic guitar, and clarinet. Although she enjoyed classical music and a lot of her degree had focused on this, Annie enjoyed playing popular music. She would frequently strum along to the latest hits, finding it easy to pick out the relevant chords. Recently, she had got to know Tom, who played in a band, and he had invited her to join their four-piece ensemble, as they were looking for a female vocalist and guitar player, since the previous singer had moved on to pastures new.

Whenever she visited Serendipity, her grandmother Anne always insisted that Annie played for them, and usually the request included *Silent Worship*, which was a firm favourite of both Nana Anne and Grandpa Jacques. Annie didn't mind playing these tunes, but tried to include some modern ones, too, much to Anne's chagrin.

On one such occasion, Jacques said, winking at Annie, 'Come on Anne, you've got to move with the times, you know!'

'I know, but you can't beat some of the classical stuff. It's been around for centuries. This modern stuff, as you call it, it will come and go along with fashion and other such fads.'

Annie didn't agree, arguing the case for the Beatles, who were increasingly famous, and making hit records some ten years after they hit the music scene.

'Yes, but they won't last as long as such composers as Handel and Chopin,' Anne argued.

Jacques decided to excuse himself, as he knew the debates between Anne and her headstrong granddaughter Annie had a habit of going on for some time. They were so alike in many ways. Apart from their love of music, they both held quite firm and sometimes opposing views on many societal matters, ranging from politics to religion. Anne still held strong beliefs about women's rights, stemming from her association with the Suffragette movement in earlier times. Annie was also a feminist, and Jacques concluded that it would take a certain type of man to suit his headstrong granddaughter.

Annie continued to sing and play in the band, appearing at venues all over England. They were getting quite a name for themselves. On one occasion, they were approached by a record producer, who offered them the chance to record one of the songs which Annie and Michael Blanchflower, the lead guitarist, had written. At first, they were a little reluctant, but Jeff, the record producer, was persuasive, offering to promote and help market the record, and so before long they had signed a contract with a record company.

Much to their surprise, their song climbed up the charts, reaching number four. They were an overnight success, and suddenly everyone wanted to speak to them. They appeared on *Top of the Pops*, as Millie, Anne, Jacques and even John watched with pride from their armchairs. Anne, now seventy-seven years old, thoroughly enjoyed Annie's band's music, which was described as Indie-Modern, and she even threatened to go to one of their concerts!

Annie and Michael wrote and recorded many more songs, and began to tour all over Britain, and then Holland, Germany and France. One of their records reached number one in February 1977, and they had the opportunity to tour in the USA. During this time, some members of the original band had left, but Annie and Michael remained the anchors for the group. Their relationship blossomed, and they decided to move in together, in a lovely, large four-bedroom house in Hertfordshire, which they had managed to purchase as a result of their successful musical careers.

Several years later, as their popularity began to wane, they continued to make records, but by this time they had married, Annie becoming Mrs Blanchflower, with a family and other commitments. The music industry of the eighties was demanding a different genre of music, and they had decided that, with three young children, touring was no longer an option, and so concentrated on teaching and developing new talent in the pop industry.

When the children were small, Annie would frequently visit Serendipity, and continued to have many heated debates with her grandmother Anne, who even in her eighties still played the piano, and occasionally the clarinet. Often when they were together with Annie's children, they would play and sing their favourite aria: *Silent Worship* by Handel, and before long the little ones would try to join in. Annie had even tried to produce a more upbeat version for the pop world, much to Anne's chagrin.

Anne lost her beloved Jacques, and the song would frequently bring tears to her eyes, while Annie and the children would try to console her, but after his death, Anne lost some of her zest for life. In later life, Jacques had developed heart problems, and it was these that led to his death. However, Anne did love to see her great-grandchildren, John, Lawrence and Rachel, who were all so young and full of life. Millie and Sean now resided at Serendipity, and poor John still ambled around the house, muttering to himself a lot of the time.

One summer's day, Anne and Annie were in the garden. The weather was clement, and the July sun warmed their faces as they sat on the garden bench. Suddenly, Anne rose and slowly began walking towards the bottom of the garden. 'Annie, follow me, I want to show you something.'

Annie dutifully followed her grandmother, wondering what she was going to show her. On reaching the back garden wall, which was covered in an overgrowth of ivy and leafy hedge, Anne began grappling with the overgrowth.

Annie thought she had flipped and demanded, 'Nan, what are you doing?!'

'Just wait and see.'

Eventually Anne managed to move some of the foliage away, to reveal an old wooden gate.

'Here it is at last!' Anne sighed, feeling quite fatigued after the effort of clearing the foliage away. 'I haven't been through this gate for a long time.'

She tried to lift the latch, which was very rusty and stiff. Annie offered to help, and eventually they managed to open the gate, which creaked with every move. As it opened, they both gazed out over the open fields, simultaneously drawing breath at the wonderful view before them. They ventured slowly through the gate, and Annie helped her grandmother to walk across the field to the babbling brook, which remained well hidden by the trees. Some of it had dried up over the years, and the area seemed more overgrown. Anne stood surveying the scene. She could feel tears pricking her eyes as she remembered when she had once danced there with Jacques.

'Are you okay, Nan?' Annie enquired, linking arms with her

grandmother. They stood there quietly for a few moments, then Anne told her granddaughter all about how she used to escape through the secret gate, to get away from her tyrannical father, and how she met up with Claudine and Jacques, and how this had changed her life. She regaled some of the adventures they had together. As she thought about Claudine, who had died the previous year, she began to feel sad again. She felt like she needed to sit down; her legs as well as her heart were heavy. Annie detected this, and suggested they return to the garden. She closed the secret gate, and Anne caught her breath as she sank down onto the garden bench.

Still quite tearful, she said, 'I have never told anyone about the secret gate, but I felt I had to share it with you.' She clasped Annie's hand as she spoke.

'Thanks, Nan,' said Annie, as she held her grandmother's hand tightly and felt a tear in her own eye.

For several years after, and for as long as Anne was able to walk, they would venture together through the secret gate, sharing their hopes and dreams, and philosophising over the complexities of life and love.

Chapter 13

Anne lived until she was ninety-four. She had even managed to play *Silent Worship*, accompanied by Annie, the Christmas before she died. The following spring, of 1992, she developed a bad chesty cold, which progressed to pneumonia. Before Anne became too poorly to venture out, Annie took her through the secret gate for the last time. They both knew it was the final time they would stand together gazing over the open fields, and they both had tears in their eyes. Annie made a promise that she would continue to go through the secret gate as long as she was able. This promise made Anne very happy.

The funeral was a sombre affair. Many of Anne's past pupils and their families attended. She had requested that *Silent Worship* be played, and there were tears in everyone's eyes, especially Annie's, as the coffin was carried from the church. Millie remained her stoic self, but during the service, when the vicar was focusing on Anne's long and musically active life, the tears were rolling down her face as she stifled a sob, thinking of the loss of a very precious mother. Anne had managed to outlive both of her sisters, Cecilia and Claire, and John was the only surviving sibling. He remained very quiet and withdrawn throughout the whole funeral service.

Serendipity seemed a much quieter place after Anne's death. Millie and Sean were both retired, and John's mental health had deteriorated to the extent that communication with him was non-existent. It was not long before he followed his sisters and brother, dying quietly at home, in his bed one night. The house seemed emptier than ever, but Annie knew instinctively what was missing. The sound of music.

On a trip through the secret gate one day, she stood in the open field, thinking of Anne and Jacques, and the life and liveliness they had brought to Serendipity with their music. She decided to make sure she played the piano each time she visited.

As the years passed, John, Lawrence and Rachel grew up happy and healthy. Unfortunately, despite having musical parents, none of them decided to have a career in music, although John did play bass guitar in an amateur band. Lawrence went to university, studying medicine, and Rachel had chosen to study for a degree in psychology. Annie and Michael continued to teach music, giving mainly private tuition from their home. They still had an interest in promoting new talent, and did a lot of this via the pupils they taught.

Sean died when he was in his late seventies, leaving Millie living alone at Serendipity. Whenever Annie visited, she was frequently told by Millie how big and rambling the house seemed for one person. She could appreciate how her mother felt. Annie's children, now older, only tended to visit at holiday times, so often she was the only visitor. She tried to encourage her mother to get out and about, but Millie suffered with osteoarthritis, which impaired her mobility.

'I'm not a youngster, you know,' Millie would say to Annie, 'I'm nearly eighty!' Annie did not like to think of her mother getting old and infirm, and she worried how Millie was coping. She shared her concerns with Michael one evening, as they sat watching TV.

'If she can't cope on her own, what happens then?'

Michael didn't respond straight away to a question; he always liked to think questions through carefully, before giving an answer. He was different to Annie in that way; she was far more impulsive. "Opposites attract" certainly applied to their relationship. It worked.

'I've got an idea. What if you and I were to move into Serendipity, and keep an eye on your mum? We could either sell or rent this house, which is really too big for the two of us, and costing us quite a lot of money to maintain.'

Annie surprised by this suggestion, but the more she thought about it, the more it made perfect sense. *Trust my sensible husband to come up with this.*

So Annie and Michael moved into Serendipity in the autumn of 2006. Although initially Millie pretended to be annoyed with this decision, when the weather became colder and there was snow and ice on the ground, she was glad of their company. The house seemed to come alive again, with frequent visits from John, and occasionally Lawrence and Rachel. Annie was tempted to tell John about the secret gate, but somehow felt that it should only be revealed to a female in the family line. She knew this wouldn't be her daughter Rachel, who had just gone off to university in Durham, where her boyfriend Liam had gone the year before. The pair were inseparable, and Annie had resigned herself to the idea that they would probably settle somewhere up north after university. She had never been that close to Rachel, being far closer to John, who shared her quirky personality and love of music. John loved visiting Serendipity. He worked as a teacher in a busy secondary school, and appreciated the peace and quiet Serendipity offered during his holidays.

Life continued quite mundanely at Serendipity. Annie still gave music lessons, and Michael had some input to a music course run by a local college. Millie became increasingly frail, and Annie noticed she was beginning to forget things. She would offer to make tea, and put the kettle on, but then she would leave the kitchen without making the tea. As a consequence, Annie was more reluctant to leave her home alone. She tried to keep Millie active, by getting her to accompany her to the shops and to walk their new little Westie puppy, Snoopy. Millie seemed to have a lot of energy for these activities, and Annie noticed she appeared more lucid when she had been out of the house. Annie also benefited from the exercise. Their relationship was probably the best it had ever been over the years, with Millie even joining in the occasional musical soirees, initiated mainly by Annie, and sometimes Michael.

When the family all got together at Christmas, there was much joy and merriment. *Silent Worship* was resurrected, and duly dedicated to

Anne and Jacques. John even played a version of it on his electric guitar, which resulted in Millie placing her fingers in her ears and shouting at the top of her voice: 'Stop that awful noise!'

This made everyone smile, except Millie. The Christmas festivities passed happily and before they knew it, New Year was being welcomed in by all the family.

'Let's hope it's a good one!' said Michael, holding Annie's hand tightly as they stood outside in the cold night air, watching the fireworks light up the dark sky.

'Yes, let's hope so!' was Annie's reply. Once the short firework display was finished, they all piled back into the house, grateful of the warm fire, which they huddled around, drinking their traditional hot toddies. Soon people started yawning and retiring to bed. Annie and Michael were the last to climb the stairs.

Such a lot has happened in this house over the years, but there has always been family solidarity... long may it continue! Annie thought, as she kissed Michael goodnight, once they were comfortably tucked up in bed.

January and February brought lots of cold, icy and windy weather, compounded on occasions by some heavy snowfalls. Unfortunately, Millie managed to slip over on the ice in the garden, and broke her hip. She was admitted to hospital, where Annie spent several days visiting her. The doctor had said it was quite a nasty break, and that she would require surgery to repair it. While she was in the hospital, one of the nurses gently approached the subject of Millie's mental health. The admission to hospital, along with the change of environment, had made her dementia worse.

'We can refer her to see a consultant for her dementia,' the nurse suggested one afternoon, when Annie had just finished visiting. The visit had been particularly distressing, as Millie didn't seem to know who she was.

Annie felt close to tears as the nurse discussed her mother. 'But what can the consultant possibly do?' she asked, anxiously clasping her handkerchief.

The friendly nurse, detecting her anxiety, placed a hand on her arm. 'Oh, there's quite a lot that can be done; not just medication, but exercises that can help with memory loss. I can arrange for you to speak to a doctor about this if you like.'

'Yes please, that would be helpful. Can I bring my husband?'

'Of course you can. Shall we see if we can arrange a convenient date and time?' And so arrangements were made, and later that week Annie and Michael spoke to a Dr Jennings, who insisted that they call her Natalie. She was very helpful, and suggested that Millie be referred to Dr Eccleston, a consultant gerontologist, who specialised in dementia.

'Dr Eccleston is wonderful. She has a lot of experience with dementia patients, and will certainly be able to help Millie,' said Dr Jennings reassuringly. Two weeks later, Millie was discharged from hospital. Her hip operation had gone well, and she had some mobility, thanks to the help of a Zimmer frame. Even so, her mental health was suffering, and she was a constant worry to her daughter.

As winter turned to spring, and the weather began to warm up, Annie decided to escape through the secret gate. She was feeling fraught, after another incident with Millie that morning. Eventually, an appointment with Dr Eccleston had been set up for the following week.

It won't come soon enough for me! Annie thought as she gazed over the open fields, in an attempt to settle her nerves. Although Michael was helpful, he was not always at Serendipity, so most of the responsibility of caring for Millie fell on her. She frequently found herself talking to her greatly missed grandmother, Anne, when walking in the open spaces. She seemed to gain some solace from this. Annie had left Millie asleep, but was conscious that she couldn't be away from the house too long, so with reluctance she finally returned. Thankfully, Millie was still asleep upstairs in her room, so Annie decided to play the piano, and before long she was playing *Silent Worship*. As she played, she felt as if Anne was there with her, and the tears began to flow freely as she reflected on happier times. Eventually, her playing was interrupted by her mobile phone ringing. It was John.

'Hi Mum, are you okay?' came John's cheery voice, Annie could feel her sombre mood lifting; she loved to hear from John.

'Yes, I'm fine, are you?'

'Yes, I'm wonderful thanks, and how's Gran?'

Annie didn't really want to discuss her mother, so quickly replied, 'Oh, she's fine.'

'Mum, could I visit this weekend, and can I bring a friend?'

'Of course you can, you don't really need to ask.'

'I know, but you and Dad may have something planned.'

'Like what – we can't really leave Millie!'

'Sorry... silly me, didn't think of that!' There seemed to be a silent pause, and then John said, 'Mum, this friend of mine is a female. I want you and Dad to meet her, as she is rather special to me.'

Annie's ears pricked up. 'You haven't mentioned anyone, please do tell me more!'

John went on to tell Annie that he had known this *female* since just after Christmas, and he was well and truly smitten. She was called Rose, and he had met her at the local gym. She was a nurse who specialised in diabetes. She was tall with blonde hair, blue eyes, and a lovely disposition. Her parents were both Irish, and she lived at home with them and her younger brother Patrick.

'I am dying for you to meet her, I know you will like her,' said John, with some anxiety in his voice.

'I'm sure we will. If you like her, then we will, too,' said Annie reassuringly. She could hear the *clomp, clomp* of Millie's Zimmer frame as she moved towards the entrance to the lounge. 'John, I must go, Gran has just appeared. Let me know the details about the weekend. Look forward to seeing you, and meeting Rose.'

'Yes, will do, bye, give my love to Gran.'

'Will do.' Annie pressed the end call button, and John was gone.

'Who are you talking to?' Millie enquired as she made her way towards a nearby armchair.

'John has just telephoned. He is coming for the weekend, and bringing his new girlfriend with him.'

Her mother looked a little vague, and Annie knew what was coming next.

'Who's John?'

Annie explained who John was, and then offered to put the TV on. The background noise often seemed to settle Millie. When she could see that her mother looked like she was going to stay put, she said, 'I'm just going to prepare tea. Michael will be home soon.'

Her mother didn't answer. She seemed to have become engrossed in an episode of *Escape to the Country*, so Annie hurried out quickly to the kitchen. Not long after, Michael appeared, and soon they were gathered around the kitchen table, tucking into sausage and mash; one of Michael's favourites.

'This is great after that long and tedious session on music theory this afternoon. It's such a dry subject to teach, and I can see a lot of the students switching off. Never mind; the morning was better, with one-to-one guitar lessons.'

This was the part of the job he enjoyed the most, as did Annie. She told him about John's news, which Michael was delighted to hear. Millie sat through the whole meal without uttering a word. Annie wondered how she would react to the presence of a stranger in the house. Her mother had become extremely wary of anyone she didn't know, and would often say inappropriate comments to them. She just hoped this wouldn't happen when John introduced Rose to his family.

Chapter 14

It was a lovely spring morning as Annie went into the garden to cut a few daffodils to brighten up the hall in preparation for the guests. John had telephoned earlier, to say they hoped to arrive around lunchtime, traffic permitting.

Luckily, Millie seemed less fraught, and was talking amicably to Michael in the lounge. Annie set out the cups and saucers for refreshments. She felt that she had to keep herself occupied, her mind racing at the thought of meeting John's new girlfriend, and hoping that Millie would behave.

Eventually, John's car pulled up in the driveway. Annie had been looking out of the window, and so promptly opened the door to greet them. She observed Rose getting out of the car. John was right, she certainly was a beauty. She was tall and elegant, and was dressed smartly in a checked blazer and dark skinny jeans, which made her slim legs look even longer. Her blonde hair was swept up in a bun, accentuating her high cheekbones and sparkling blue eyes, which one could not help but notice. She strode purposefully towards Annie, with an outstretched hand.

'Hello, Mrs Blanchflower, it's lovely to meet you.'

Annie clasped Rose's hand. It felt cool. 'Lovely to meet you too, do come in and warm yourself.'

Rose went into the house, and was met by Michael, who directed her towards the lounge. John followed suit, and soon they were all sipping tea and nibbling biscuits. The journey hadn't been without incident.

Rose said there had been a pile-up on the motorway and so part of the lanes had been closed off. There were two ambulances and some police cars at the site, and several smashed-up cars.

'We were so lucky that we weren't caught up in it,' said John, as he reached for Rose's hand.

'You certainly were,' said Annie, offering to make more tea. She was aware that Millie had sat quietly through all the conversation. As if Rose had read her mind, she began to talk gently to Millie. At first, Millie was a bit wary, but as Rose explained who she was, and why she was there, Millie began to open up, and actually smiled at Rose. Annie had not seen her mother smile for such a long time, she had to wipe a tear from her eye as she observed the two of them. Michael, who was also observing the interaction, smiled knowingly at Annie.

The rest of the day passed very harmoniously. Rose and Millie seemed to be getting on like a house on fire, with Rose offering to take Millie to her room for her afternoon nap. Annie felt so grateful for this unexpected gesture. After they left the room, John turned nervously to Annie and said, 'So what do you think of Rose?'

'She seems very nice; so natural, and very pretty, too!'

'Yes, I have to agree, you've got a very special lady there,' said Michael.

'I know, that's why I wanted you to meet her.' John was smiling as he said this. 'I can't believe it sometimes, she is almost too good to be true!' Going a little quiet, Annie could tell John wanted to say more; she recognised that look.

'Come on, what else is on your mind?'

John looked up at her, still smiling. 'I have asked her to move in with me, and she has said yes!'

Annie wasn't quite expecting this but said, 'I see. So when does all this happen?'

Rose returned to the lounge, so the conversation was cut short. She informed them that Millie had fallen asleep almost straight away.

'Yes, she seems to get so tired these days,' said Annie.

'I think having dementia does tend to make sufferers very tired,' said Rose with empathy. She went on to tell them about her grandfather, who had suffered with dementia. 'He lived over in Ireland, so we didn't see him that much, but my Aunt Colleen, who kept an eye on him, used to tell us that he was always very tired.'

Feeling she had an ally in Rose, Annie opened up about Millie, stressing her concern about her mother's future deterioration. By this time, Michael and John had retreated to the garden, leaving the ladies to chat.

'It can be a very slow process, I believe,' said Rose, relaxing back in her armchair.

Annie went on to discuss how difficult it was at times, keeping a close eye on her mother. 'It's like having a two-year-old!'

Rose nodded in agreement. It felt really good to Anne, to be able to discuss her mother with someone who seemed to understand. She felt like she was sharing some of the burden.

'Can you not get someone to come and sit with Millie, so you can have a break?' Rose suggested. Annie had not considered this as an option, and said so.

'I'm sure if you contact your GP, or even speak to the practice nurse, there are nurse or care agencies, and they can provide a suitable carer to enable you to have some time off.'

Annie felt heartened by this suggestion, and promised she would speak to their GP very soon.

The evening meal took place later in the day. Annie and Michael did all the cooking themselves; long gone were the times when there was a housekeeper or cook at Serendipity. They all gathered around the dining room table, and tucked into lamb steaks with chips and mixed vegetables, followed by a raspberry pavlova with cream. Rose complimented Annie on the latter.

'It's delicious, you must let me have the recipe,' said Rose, as she cleared the last spot of cream from her plate.

'It's from one of Mary Berry's recipe books,' Annie informed her.

The evening passed amicably, with plenty of chatter, ranging from current news items to the latest music scene. John continued to play in his band at least twice a month, with Rose frequently attending the gigs. She praised John's group, implying that they had the potential to become professionals. John appeared quite embarrassed by all the praise from Rose and said, 'You never know, maybe I will follow in my parents' footsteps after all, and become famous!!'

Millie suddenly began to laugh. Rose asked her calmly what was so funny, to which she replied, 'Him being famous? That's a joke. Have you heard that din he plays on that guitar of his?!'

John began to chuckle at this, and the others joined in, including Millie.

Annie had not seen her mother so happy for a long time. 'You must come again, Rose. You have certainly put a smile on Mum's face!'

'I would love to come again, you have all made me feel so welcome,' said Rose, smiling from ear to ear. Annie felt a warm glow inside as she served the coffee to her close-knit family. She decided that Rose was already part of that family, and told her so.

Rose and John were tired after their journey, and decided to retire to bed quite early. Annie had automatically set up two separate rooms for them, since there were plenty of empty bedrooms at Serendipity. They had dropped their luggage earlier in these rooms. As they left the room, John beckoned Annie into the hallway. Rose had already begun to climb the stairs, yawning. In a low voice, he said, 'Mum, how do you feel about Rose and me sharing a bedroom?'

Annie was not entirely surprised by this question. 'It's up to you – you're both grown adults.'

'I know, but this is yours and Dad's house, and we want to respect your wishes while staying here.'

'That's very thoughtful of you both. But go ahead and decide which room you want.'

'Thanks Mum, you're a star!' John kissed her on the cheek and ascended the stairs two at a time.

There won't be much sleeping going on with them tonight! Annie thought as she detected the spring in John's footsteps. Once back in the lounge, she relayed the story to Michael, who found it all rather amusing. Millie just seemed to be staring into space as Annie and Michael laughed together.

About an hour later, they also retired to bed, Annie helping her mother to undress and get into bed. She spoke quietly to Millie, 'What do you think of Rose?'

'Who's Rose?'

'You know, the young lady with John. She's tall and slim with lovely blonde hair.'

'Oh, that lady – she's very nice.' Millie smiled as she responded and once in bed seemed to fall asleep very quickly.

As she got into bed beside Michael, who was already asleep, Annie pondered on the day's events. All had gone very well, and she felt she had found a new friend in Rose, who was the epitome of an angel in disguise. *I bet she is an excellent nurse.*

Annie fell into a contented slumber, looking forward to the next day.

A Sunday lunch of roast lamb, with roast potatoes and a selection of vegetables, was heartily consumed, partly because the lunch had been preceded by a walk around the local area. The weather was quite cold but sunny, and the exercise was enjoyed by one and all. Rose had nothing but praise for the surrounding countryside.

'It reminds me of my grandfather's place in Ireland. He lived in a farmhouse, not too far from the main road, which was surrounded by miles and miles of open countryside. My brother and I used to wander round the fields for hours, enjoying the freedom of just roaming around. Somehow, you felt safe.' Annie listened to Rose's tale, and wondered if she should share the secret gate with her, but hastily decided that it was too soon.

The homemade apple pie, John's favourite, was gratefully eaten, with Annie offering to give the remainder to John to take home with him. This action had become a bit of a ritual over the years. It made Rose laugh, and Millie joined in with her.

All too soon, it was time for Rose and John to depart. They packed quickly and, following a fifteen-minute slot of goodbyes, and promises to return again soon, John was driving the car onto the road. Annie and Michael looked forward to their next visit.

Spring moved on to summer and, taking Rose's advice, Annie managed to arrange for a carer to come and sit with Millie, to give her and

Michael a break. Jenny came once a week on a Friday, and had bonded very well with Millie. She had a vivacious personality, which seemed to work with Millie's normally rather sombre disposition. Jenny had also kindly offered to do some housework whilst she tended to Millie. It made a huge difference to Annie, to have her help. One day, Annie and Michael returned from an afternoon spent relaxing at a local National Trust property, and found Millie helping Jenny with the dusting. They were both singing merrily in the lounge, unaware that they were no longer alone. Annie recognised the song from the musical *South Pacific*, and found herself joining in.

Rose and John visited in July, with the news of their plans to marry the following summer. Everyone congratulated them; even Millie.

'Millie seems happier,' Rose commented to Annie when they were alone in the kitchen.

'I think some of it is due to Jenny.'

'Who's Jenny?'

'She's the carer who comes every Friday.'

'I'm so glad. It must be nice for you to have a break.'

'Yes, it is. We're planning to have a weekend away in September, as Jenny said she would be happy to take care of Millie for us.'

'That will do you both good,' said Rose, as they made their way into the lounge to join the others. Annie observed how well John and Rose got on, and there seemed to be an inner contentment, similar to what she and Michael shared. She was very happy for them.

As always, their short visit passed quickly, and soon they were on their way home again. They had met Jenny, and Rose had commented favourably about her happy, fun-loving disposition, which was just what Millie needed.

Millie seemed sad to see them go, and stood on the doorstep, waving them off. Sometimes, she seemed quite lucid, but would then forget where she was, or who anyone was. Annie often wondered how it would all end.

Chapter 15

Annie and Michael managed to have their weekend away. They decided to visit Sidmouth; a regency style seaside resort in East Devon. Staying at a comfortable four-star hotel, they relaxed and enjoyed their time out from the usual routine. Michael had been working extra hours to cover for a colleague's sick leave, and Annie had been quite busy giving music lessons at Serendipity, so they were both in need of rejuvenation. Although Annie did have a break from Millie when Jenny came, she had to watch her mother for most of each day, except when she was asleep. As Millie had become more agitated, the GP had put her on medication, which made her increasingly tired. Annie felt Millie was slowly deteriorating, and when she discussed this with both Michael and Jenny, they agreed.

As the autumn winds began to blow, Annie had escaped through the secret gate, taking in the view of the scattered golden leaves in the fields, and contemplating the progressive change to the trees and hedgerows. It was late October, and earlier that day, Millie had decided to take her skirt and jumper off and parade around the back garden in her underwear. She said she had gone out to collect the fallen apples, to make some apple pie. This had caused Annie to inwardly smile, as her mother had never been interested in baking.

Rose and John visited one weekend in November, and Annie confided in Rose about her concerns for Millie. Rose had to admit that she did seem to be worse. She no longer smiled at Rose, and even Jenny couldn't get through. Millie was gradually retreating into a world of her own, and there seemed nothing that could be done about it. At one stage, she was still able to recognise her husband Sean in photos, but now she didn't even know who he was. It made Annie very sad to see her mother like this. Rose tried to comfort her, which was greatly appreciated by Annie, who was beginning to wonder how Christmas would pan out.

Christmas duly arrived, and all the family got together. Annie was very busy Christmas morning, preparing the lunch. Rose had very kindly offered to help her, and this was much appreciated. It also gave them a chance to chat about Millie. There had been several incidents leading up to Christmas, when Millie had become very aggressive, and had even punched poor Jenny as she had tried to calm her down. She had also managed to slip on the ice out in the garden, and had grazed the side of her face quite badly. This had happened very recently, and all the family agreed that she looked like she had been in World War Three! Annie told Rose that she didn't know how much longer she could cope with her mother.

'You need more help,' Rose said as she helped prepare the brussels sprouts.

'I think I do, but what help can be provided?'

'You must go back to your GP again, and explain the situation.'

'They know about Mum's fall, as I had to have the doctor out to check she was okay. I tried to tell the visiting doctor how difficult things were getting, but he didn't seem to be interested. I think he just wanted to get on, and see his next patient.'

'Oh dear, that's not helpful.' Michael entered the kitchen to get some drinks for Rachel and Lawrence, who had just arrived. The conversation was cut short as Annie went out to greet them. They both looked so grown up, it made Annie feel quite old as she hugged them both.

The tasty Christmas lunch was heartily enjoyed by all, and, feeling full but contented, they retired to the lounge to watch the Queen's speech on TV. Rose had kindly offered to take Millie off to bed. Luckily, Annie's mother had been very quiet over lunch, only muttering to herself most of the time. After the Queen's speech, Annie, Michael, John and Rose decided to venture out for a walk. Although it was cold, the sun was shining, and the sky was clear blue. They chatted about the plans for Rose and John's wedding. The date had now been set for the end of July, and the honeymoon was in hand. John was keeping the destination a secret from Rose.

Annie felt quite relaxed as they returned to Serendipity, but alas, this was to be short-lived. Whilst they were out, Millie had woken up and come downstairs, ranting and raving, and calling out Annie's name. She wanted to know who Lawrence and Rachel were, and when they tried to calm her down, she had grabbed hold of poor Rachel's hair, which was hanging loosely over her shoulders, pulling it hard, and Lawrence had to physically prise her off, then attempt to get her to sit down. Millie promptly decided to venture out into the garden, and had since refused to come in. There were tears in poor Rachel's eyes as she recovered from her encounter.

'How long has she been outside?' Annie asked as she headed for the back garden, with the others in hot pursuit.

'Oh-h not long, probably only about five minutes,' said Lawrence, following them out into the garden. 'I tried to get her to come in, but she told me to get lost, and to leave her alone!"

'Oh dear,' said Rose, placing a comforting hand on Lawrence's arm. He was clearly unnerved.

Annie tried to reason with Millie, in an attempt to coax her back indoors, as the sun was starting to recede in the sky, and the temperature was dropping. Millie was having none of it. Annie could feel her frustration rising as Michael too tried to talk Millie round. Rose started walking slowly towards Millie, talking very softly to her, until eventually she was able to take her hand, and lead her gingerly back into the house. Everyone breathed a sigh of relief.

Once in the kitchen, Annie made them all some tea, and even Millie drank hers with relish. She began to yawn, clearly tired after her flare-up, so Annie decided to take her off to bed. Once in Millie's room, she helped her mother to undress, and then tucked her into bed. She kissed her cold cheek, and left the room. Annie felt like bursting into tears as she descended the stairs to join the others in the lounge. *How much longer can this go on?* she asked herself.

The remainder of the day passed peacefully, although the mood was somewhat tainted by the earlier episode. Rachel hadn't spoken at all, and Lawrence had engrossed himself on his iPhone. Annie was feeling guilty, because she had selfishly gone out, and left them to mind Millie.

The TV was on, but Annie was not really paying attention, her mind focused on her mother's earlier behaviour. Eventually, she suggested they all had a glass of wine, which resulted in a resounding 'yes' from everyone. The TV seemed to improve, with an old Morecambe & Wise Christmas show, which had everyone smiling; even Rachel. Eventually, the family began to retire to bed, leaving just Rose and Annie to clear up the glasses, and dispose of the empty wine bottles. Rose asked if she was okay, and Annie burst into tears – it had all been too much for her, and she collapsed down on the kitchen chair.

Rose was at her side immediately, placing a reassuring arm around her. 'Sometimes, we need a good cry to get it all out of our system... it can work wonders!'

Annie nodded in agreement as the tears continued to flow. She cried for about five minutes in all, and had to admit she did feel better. They decided to have a night cap of whisky and hot water, and then both went up the stairs to bed, feeling slightly drunk, but ready for sleep. On reaching her bedroom, Annie turned to Rose, and gave her a big hug. 'Thanks for all your support, and just for listening.'

'No problem – anytime,' whispered Rose.

They parted company, and retired for the night. Annie slept like a baby, and woke the next morning feeling quite refreshed, despite a slight niggling headache. Michael was already up. Getting out of bed somewhat reluctantly, Annie pulled on her warm, fleecy dressing gown. Descending the stairs, she could hear chatter coming from the kitchen. They were all in there, including Millie. Annie could smell toast.

'Good morning!' they said in unison. Rose poured Annie some tea, and asked if she wanted toast. Annie nodded, and shortly a slice was put in front of her.

'I could get use to this!' she said, nodding at Michael, as she spread marmalade on her warm toast.

'Could you?!' They smiled at each other.

Then Millie, staring blankly at Annie, said, 'Who is this woman?'

'It's Annie, your daughter,' said Rose.

'Oh,' was Millie's brief reply, and she carried on eating her toast.

Here we go again, Annie thought to herself, detecting Rose's mutual awareness.

The others don't seem to notice! But perhaps they do, and don't know how to deal with it, and so try to ignore it. She glanced around the table. Now everyone was silently eating their breakfast. She noticed Rachel had tied her hair up in a bun. Lawrence was reading the paper. Rose and John were sipping their tea, and Michael was yawning. Everyone seemed quite jaded, almost certainly thanks in part to Millie's little outburst yesterday. They had all planned to have a Boxing Day lunch at a nearby pub, as Jenny had very kindly agreed to mind Millie. Annie had bought Jenny a Christmas present, to show her appreciation of how well she cared for Millie, and planned to give it to her today.

Jenny, reliable as ever, arrived in plenty of time, so Annie was able to give her the present. She was a little embarrassed receiving the gift, but ripping open the wrapping paper and seeing her favourite chocolates bought a big smile to her face. Typical of Jenny, she opened the box and offered them all around. Everyone declined, except Millie, who grabbed the chocolate out of the box as if her life depended on it. This action made everyone smile before they donned their hats and coats to venture out into the cold for the ten-minute walk to the pub.

They had a delicious lunch, and the atmosphere was very relaxed. They would have liked to stay longer, but Annie was aware that she didn't want to leave Millie with Jenny for too long, particularly after yesterday's escapade. She suggested that the others stay longer, whilst she and Rose, who had offered to accompany her, went back to Serendipity. The weather had warmed slightly from the earlier winter chill, and there was a weak, watery sun in the sky; it looked like it could rain.

As they reached the house, Jenny opened the door to them talking in a low voice. 'She's just gone to sleep.'

They breathed a sigh of relief. Soon, Jenny was making them some tea, as they sat around the kitchen table.

'Let me make that,' said Annie. 'You sit down and rest. We've all been enjoying ourselves at the pub while you've been minding Millie.'

'Oh, I don't mind,' said Jenny, 'Millie's been no trouble.'

Annie and Rose smiled knowingly to each other, then proceeded to tell Jenny all about Millie's behaviour the day before.

The remainder of the Christmas and New Year break passed uneventfully, and as they welcomed in 2008, Annie wondered, partly in trepidation, what this year would bring. Everyone had remained in quite a sombre mood, although John did offer to play the traditional *Silent Worship*. Annie, rather reluctantly, agreed to play the accompanying piano, but couldn't bring herself to sing. She could feel a lump rising in her throat as she played the tune. Rose detected her sadness, and tactfully went on to suggest they play a game of Cluedo. Her suggestion was gladly accepted by all.

All too soon, it was time for the family to leave Serendipity, and head back to their respective lives. Lawrence was giving Rachel a lift back to university, where she would catch up with her boyfriend. So they left first, followed by Rose and John. Rose thanked Annie and Michael for their hospitality over the festive season, saying how they had enjoyed the break.

Annie laughed and said, 'Even with Mum's little outburst?!'

'Yes, that was the main event!' said John, giving Annie a hug.

Rose gave her a hug too, and with a knowing nod said, 'Please do let us know if we can help with anything. Even if you just need to chat to someone, give us a ring, won't you?'

'Of course we will.' Annie was so grateful to Rose for her understanding and help with Millie, and she felt slightly bereft as Rose and John drove off.

Sensing this, Michael took hold of her hand, saying, 'We'll get through this – don't worry.'

January and February passed with the winter taking hold with cold, sharp frosts, and some downpours of snow. Millie seemed to quieten down once her medication had been changed. Jenny continued to visit on a Friday, and overall life was quite mundane. On a couple of occasions, Annie managed to escape through the secret gate, where she sought the peace and tranquillity the wide-open spaces offered her. Sometimes, she would play the piano, and one day decided to play the flute, which she had not played for quite some time. She was just embarking on a rendition of Mozart's *Rondo alla Turca* when her mother suddenly appeared, ranting and raving, and telling her to stop playing immediately. The sound of the flute had clearly upset her, so Annie promptly stopped playing.

Several minutes later, she had managed to calm her mother down, and they both sat quietly in the lounge. Annie put the TV on, as this seemed to focus Millie's attention, and soon she became absorbed watching one of the game shows.

Later that day, Annie told Michael about the incident. She found such occurrences very stressful, and quite exhausting. Millie was due to see the GP soon, to assess her dementia. They both wondered what the outcome would be.

Following the GP's assessment, it became evident that Millie was deteriorating further.

'She may need to go into a home when you feel you can no longer cope,' Dr Jones had suggested tactfully.

'What about Millie attending a day centre?' Michael asked.

'Yes, that is a possibility. Do you want me to make some enquiries?'

They had both agreed, and Dr Jones said he would keep them informed.

Springtime arrived, and the weather slowly began to warm up. Annie had heard nothing yet about day care for Millie. Her mother's condition continued to deteriorate, and so Annie decided to contact the GP for another appointment. Dr Jones explained that he had sent a referral to the nearest day centre, but had not received a reply. He promised to chase it up.

Rose and John visited briefly at Easter, and they could both see that Millie was getting worse. She rarely spoke, and most of the time seemed to be in her own world, muttering unintelligible words to herself. She didn't know who anybody was, and was constantly walking around the house as if searching for something. Then she would go to bed, with Annie's assistance, and sleep. Annie was grateful for this respite, and on occasions found herself dropping off from sheer exhaustion.

Chapter 16

It was early May, and Annie was in the garden, sitting on the bench and enjoying the warmth of the sun on her face. She had been doing some weeding whilst Millie was asleep. Feeling exhausted after a disturbed night, with her mother wandering around the house at 2am, Annie's eyes gradually shut, and she fell into a much-needed slumber.

She was awakened by the sound of someone shouting and banging frantically on the front door of the house. With a jolt, Annie jumped up from the bench and she nearly tumbled over, as she moved quickly through the house to the front door. She could see two figures through the frosted glass. Opening the door, she was greeted by her neighbour, Mrs Stokes, and another person whom she did not know. When she saw the expressions on their faces, she knew something was wrong.

Mrs Stokes began to speak. 'Annie, it's your mother, I'm afraid. She's been knocked down by a car.'

'Oh my god, is she alright?' Annie pushed past them, and saw her mother lying still in the road. There was blood oozing from her head. Annie raced over to Millie and, falling to her knees, she began frantically calling her mother's name. There was no response. Mrs Stokes tried to pull Annie away, but she refused to move. The car that had knocked Millie down was nowhere to be seen. Apparently, the driver had just driven away without stopping.

'We called the ambulance as soon as we heard the screech of car brakes, and we are informed they are on their way.' Right on cue, an ambulance with flashing lights appeared. It promptly pulled up, and a paramedic swiftly emerged, carrying equipment. He kindly asked everyone to stand back while he assessed the situation.

By this time, a police car had also arrived, and traffic control was in place. Annie felt like she was in a bad dream, as she took in all the activity. The paramedic had a serious expression on his face as he began to deal with Millie. The blood was still oozing from her head, and she looked deathly pale. He covered her in a blanket, and soon he was joined by his colleague. Annie noticed how petite the woman was; she looked too small to be carrying such a lot of heavy equipment. She was vaguely aware that the paramedic was saying something to Mrs Stokes, and one of the policemen had joined them. They approached Annie. Their expressions were sombre.

It was the paramedic who spoke. 'Hello, I'm Patricia. Am I right in assuming that you are the daughter?'

'Y- yes I am,' she said. 'Is my mum all right?'

'Can we go inside?' said Patricia, pointing towards the house. Annie led the way in, and they assembled in the lounge.

'You may like to sit down,' Patricia suggested. They all promptly sat down, and then Patricia said, 'I'm sorry to tell you that your mother is dead. The impact from the car has resulted in her sustaining severe head and chest injuries. I'm sorry there was nothing we could do.' Annie could hear someone screaming. It was all so surreal. She became aware that the sound was coming from her. Mrs Stokes was placing a comforting arm around her, while Patricia and the policeman looked on with stoic expressions. Annie felt herself shaking uncontrollably.

'My husband... we must contact my husband!' she said, grasping Mrs Stokes' arm tightly.

'Of course – how can we contact him?'

Annie tried to answer, but her brain was befuddled.

'Do you have a mobile?' Mrs Stokes asked. Annie nodded. 'Is Michael's number on it?'

'Y-y-yes.' Annie was trying to remember where her phone was, but Mrs Stokes had spotted it on the lounge table.

'Here it is. Do you want me to speak to Michael?'

'Yes please, if you don't mind.'

'I'll go and make some tea as well.' Mrs Stokes left the room, carrying the mobile. Patricia excused herself, and Annie was left with the nameless policeman, who avoided eye contact with her. Annie surveyed him briefly, concluding that he didn't look very old, and his lack of experience was evident. She tried to collect her thoughts. It was like a nightmare from which she couldn't escape. She needed Michael as soon as possible.

Some minutes later, Mrs Stokes returned with the tea, and informed Annie that Michael was on his way home. There was a light tap on the front door, and Mrs Stokes let Patricia in. Annie could hear them talking in the hall. Patricia sat down opposite Annie and said, 'We will take your mother to the hospital. You can follow us down to the hospital when your husband arrives.'

'Okay,' Annie answered. The young policeman left with Patricia, and Mrs Stokes sat in silence with Annie, while they both sipped their tea. About twenty minutes later, Michael arrived. He went straight to Annie and embraced her. She clung to him, the tears starting to flow as they both took in the enormity of the event. Mrs Stokes tactfully excused herself, telling them that if they needed any help with anything, to please let her know. Michael thanked her and, closing the door, he returned to Annie. She was still stunned.

'We'd better go down to the hospital,' Michael suggested gently.

'Yes, we'd better,' was Annie's automatic reply.

Michael gathered a few things together, and then drove slowly to the hospital. As usual, parking was difficult, but eventually they found a parking place. They were unsure as to where to go once inside the hospital, so, leaving Annie sitting in the waiting area, Michael enquired at the reception desk. The receptionist gave them some directions, and they made their way to the mortuary. On arrival, further enquiries were made, and eventually a nurse escorted them into a room where Millie's body lay. Once inside the dimly lit room, the nurse slowly uncovered the sheet, to reveal Millie's ashen face. She then swiftly exited, leaving them to say their goodbyes.

As Annie observed her mother, she thought that Millie looked peaceful at last. She gently stroked her mother's face, as her tears rolled freely. Although she felt very sad, she was relieved for poor Millie, who would no longer be a tortured soul. Annie kissed her mum's cold forehead and whispered, 'Goodbye, Mum. I love you, and I hope you are now at peace.'

Michael clasped Annie's hand, and they stood in silence for some minutes, then slowly left the room.

When they returned to Serendipity, Michael informed John and Rose, Lawrence and Rachel of Millie's death. Very soon, the phone was ringing, and text messages were pinging backwards and forwards as the news reached all the family. Annie told Michael to contact Jenny, as she was due to come and sit with Millie the next day.

That evening felt very strange, without Millie's mumblings and wanderings. Annie felt almost compelled to pop into Millie's room, to see if she was alright. She hardly slept all night, despite the consumption of a few whiskeys. She kept reliving, over and over, the day's disastrous events. Her head was full of disjointed thoughts: *If only I hadn't fallen asleep... how did she manage to get out of the front door? I must have forgotten to lock it... I hope she is at peace now...*

The morning couldn't come soon enough for Annie, as she sat drinking tea in the kitchen at 4.30am. She could hear the dawn chorus from the birds outside. At 6am, Michael joined her, and they both sat in silence, lost in their own thoughts. He had to contact work, to arrange some compassionate leave with his manager, who luckily was very understanding, having recently lost her own father.

The funeral was arranged a week later, and all the family attended. It was a quiet affair, with no reference being made to Millie's dementia during the service, or afterwards at the funeral tea at Serendipity.

The weeks passed very slowly after Millie's death. The police visited, to inform them that the person driving the car that had accidentally killed Millie had eventually turned up at the police station, and owned up to knocking Millie down They were feeling terrible, even though they were not at fault. It appeared that Millie had suddenly stepped out in front of the car, and the driver had been unable to stop.

'It will haunt the driver for the rest of his life,' said the police sergeant, as he sipped the tea Annie had made for him and his female colleague.

After they left, Annie decided to escape through the secret gate, for the first time since her mother's death. The weather was very warm for late May. She watched a crow flying swiftly through the sky, before landing on the high branch of an oak tree. The branch wavered slightly under the weight of the bird. The sky was an azure blue, dotted with wispy white clouds that floated aimlessly by. It reflected how she felt; since Millie's death, it was like she was floating through life. The intensiveness of the care her mother had needed had been replaced with nothing – she had no goals to achieve. Her time was all her own, but she didn't know what to do with it. Occasionally, she would play an instrument, but found no solace from an activity she had used to love.

She had kept in touch with Jenny, who occasionally popped round. Annie enjoyed her flamboyant personality and jovial company, and always felt cheered after she left. She had also spoken several times on the phone to Rose and John, who promised to visit soon. Michael had noticed Annie's mood, and suggested that they have a weekend away somewhere, for a change of scenery. Annie agreed, and arrangements were made for them to visit Sidmouth. They planned to stay at the same hotel four-star hotel as before.

Rose and John visited soon after Annie's and Michael's weekend away. Annie felt much restored after the break, and found her spirits lifting as she looked forward to seeing her favourite son and his future wife. Their stay, although short, was packed with activities related to the couple's forthcoming wedding in late July. They were marrying at Rose's local Catholic church, and at breakfast she was busy telling Annie about the parish priest. The weather was clement, so they were breakfasting on the patio. Michael and John were in the garden.

'Father Jacob is a bit of a joker, and is bound to come out with something funny at the wedding.'

'That should make it interesting,' said Annie, munching her croissant. She espied a small sparrow hovering close by, waiting for a crumb to fall. To oblige the waiting bird, she flicked the final crumb onto the pathway, and the bird swiftly picked it up in its beak and flew off. Annie had begun to while away many peaceful hours in the garden, observing the activity of the birds, and gaining much solace from them. She had even taken to writing a song dedicated to them, and conveyed this information to Rose, who said that she would love to hear the song sometime, so Annie promised that once she had finished it, she would play it for Rose and John.

'Perhaps I could play it at your wedding?' said Annie.

'That would be nice. John and I had wanted to ask you if you would play at the church service?'

'Go on. What would you like me to play?'

'That one you usually play at Christmas, about a lady singing in the garden, I think it's by Handel?'

This description made Annie smile,

'Oh, you mean *Silent Worship*.'

'Yes, that's the one.' Rose was smiling, too.

Annie felt quite touched by this request; the aria always held a special place in her heart, because of its connections with her grandmother Anne, so she gladly agreed to play the tune, as requested. Later that morning, John embraced his mother warmly, thanking her and saying her version would be much better than his electric guitar rendition. They recalled how Millie had squealed out loud in protest when he had played it before, and for the first time since her mother's death, Annie felt truly able to smile.

Once again, and all too soon, it was time for Rose and John to leave. As they bid each other goodbye, they realised the next time they would meet was likely to be at the wedding. John and Rose promised to keep in touch, and to update Annie and Michael regularly on all the wedding arrangements.

As they waved them off, Annie felt a sense of excitement for the forthcoming event.

Chapter 17

On 28th July 2008, at 12 midday, Rose and John were married at Corpus Christi Catholic Church. It was a glorious day, with the sun shining brightly in the cerulean blue, cloudless sky. Rose looked beautiful in her ivory wedding dress, the elongated style emphasising her tall and slim frame. Her mop of blonde hair was swept up in a bun, and decorated with soft pink petals, which matched her bouquet. John looked smart in a light-grey wedding suit and top hat, as did Michael and Patrick, Rose's father. Rose's best friend Sophie was her only bridesmaid. She looked equally stunning, in a rose-pink satin dress similar in style to Rose's. Sophie was also tall, with copper coloured hair, which contrasted superbly with her dress. Annie stood back, admiring them all as the photographer requested various poses for the wedding album. Lawrence was busy filming the whole event, and Rachel and boyfriend Liam were taking photos of everyone using their mobiles. Annie even got roped into a few poses with them.

I expect it will be those two next she thought as she watched Rachel and Liam together. They had known each other since school, and had even decided to go to the same university so they would not lose touch. Annie was glad for them, as they seemed to fit together very well, just like a pair of old gloves – just like her and Michael.

The wedding reception was at a nearby hotel. The proprietor was a distant cousin of Rose's mother, so had made a special effort to ensure everything was perfect. The meal was scrumptious, and all the wedding speeches went well, partly due to all the speakers being well supplied with plenty of fizzy wine.

It became evident from Patrick's speech that he was slightly inebriated, as he kept repeating the phrase: 'What a wonderful daughter she is, John is a lucky man.' In the end, he was instructed by his wife Colleen to please sit down and let someone else speak!

The remainder of the day passed with much laughter and frivolity. Rose and John were staying at the hotel overnight, going off on their honeymoon the next day. Rose still did not know where they were going, as John had wanted to surprise her.

Annie chatted with Colleen, who complimented her musical accompaniment at the church service. She asked Annie about the significance of the tune, and Annie explained about her grandmother, and how the tune had been passed down through the generations.

'That's really lovely,' said Colleen.

'Yes, I suppose it is.' *Silent Worship* had stayed with the family for three generations now. She was touched that John had wanted to carry on the tradition, and hoped that Anne, Jacques and Millie, wherever they were, would appreciate it, too.

Slowly, the wedding group began to disperse and make their way home. Rose and John had requested that their parents join them in the hotel lounge before they left. Colleen, Patrick, Annie and Michael gathered as requested, and Rose and John handed both sets of parents a present. This gesture was most unexpected, but gratefully received. Annie felt slightly in awe as she opened the well wrapped and wonderfully decorated gift. She opened the box to reveal a lovely crystal vase. It sparkled brightly in the daylight, and on closer inspection, Annie could see that Rose's and John's names were engraved in the glass, along with their wedding date.

'Oh, this is wonderful!' Annie exclaimed.

Colleen and Patrick had been given the same gift, and were equally pleased.

'We just wanted to give you these vases as a reminder of this wonderful day and to show our gratitude to our wonderful parents,' said Rose, looking a bit teary-eyed as she spoke. John held her hand tenderly, and everyone cheered.

It has been a wonderful day – perfect in every way, Annie thought as she finished drinking her tea and observed her son and new daughter-in-law.

The next morning, Rose and John were preparing to leave the hotel and go on honeymoon. Rose had asked John at breakfast, 'Are you going to tell me where we are going?'

John had smiled. 'You will find out very soon!' he answered smugly.

As they returned to their room, the destination was finally revealed. John handed Rose an envelope, which she quickly opened and inside was a typed invitation. It read:

John Michael Blanchflower requests the company of Rose Anne Blanchflower (nee O'Malley) for a two-week honeymoon in Sorrento, Italy.

Rose clapped her hands in glee when she read the invitation. Sorrento was her favourite place in the whole world. She had holidayed a lot in Italy, having visited Rome, Venice, Florence, and Verona. She hugged John. 'It's a good job that I have packed summer clothes, as it will be very hot.'

'I knew you wouldn't want to go anywhere cold!' John said, gazing lovingly at Rose. He was looking forward to spending two whole weeks with his new wife, undisturbed by any other commitments.

'Do Mum and Dad know where we are going?'

'Oh yes, both them and my parents were sworn to secrecy.'

Once they had packed and had checked out of the hotel, they made their way to the airport and, whilst waiting in the departure lounge Rose sent a text message to both sets of parents:

Hi all, in departure lounge – can't wait 2 fly off 2 sunny Sorrento!! Thanks again 4 the wonderful wedding day xxxxxxxx

Annie could hear her mobile 'pinging', alerting her that someone had sent a text message. She was busy trying to do the crossword in the

Sunday paper, so was grateful for the distraction. She opened the message and was pleased to see it was from her new daughter-in-law. The message made her smile. She promptly replied:

Have a super time! Glad you enjoyed your wedding – it was a wonderful day. love Mum xxxxxxx

Annie pressed the send button. She was still quite a novice at sending text messages, and was not familiar with all the predictive texting that people spoke of. Michael's skills were similar to hers, and they managed to muddle through together. She often thought that mobile phones were taking over the world, as she noticed so many people playing with them whenever she was out anywhere. *The art of conversation is definitely dying!* she would think to herself when she observed the total lack of verbal communication between these people, as they clung with almost desperation to their mobiles.

Whenever she spoke to Michael about this, he agreed. 'You see all the students at college, and even a lot of the staff, texting constantly.'

'They'll have problems with their fingers in the future, with all this texting,' would be Annie's reply.

As the summer came to an end, and the weather began to turn autumnal, Annie turned her attention to the garden. She gathered in the apples from the orchard, and had taken to baking apple pies, spurred on by the *Great British Bake Off* on TV. The pies were gratefully consumed by Michael, so Annie had been motivated to start baking cakes, instead of buying them from the supermarket. When she baked, she usually did something for Jenny, who she still saw on a regular basis. She was aware that this tendency to consume homemade cakes had to be curtailed slightly to prevent middle-age spread. Annie had already noticed an increase in her girth, and was joking about it one day with Jenny.

'I'll have to stop eating all these nice fattening cakes, they aren't good for the waistline!'

Jenny launched a response, 'Well it's too late for me!' she said as she patted her rotund tummy. They both laughed.

Annie really enjoyed her time with Jenny, as they always ended up having a hearty laugh about something. Annie had taken to playing music for Jenny, who would hum along appreciatively. Spurred on by these encounters, Annie had begun to play all her instruments again, although she couldn't bring herself to play the flute, as it reminded her so much of Millie. Whenever she ventured out through the secret gate, she found herself reflecting on those stressful times spent with her mother. She would chat to Millie, asking for her forgiveness for not minding her on that fateful day. Gradually, the memories of that awful day were fading, and Annie was sure that these soliloquies were helping her to cope.

By late November, the weather was really turning cold and frosty. Michael was busy scraping ice off the windscreen one morning before setting off for work. Annie waved him off, still in her dressing gown. She was giving a piano lesson later that morning, so once dressed she began to tune the piano in preparation. Her pupil was a fourteen-year-old girl called Claudine. She was very musically talented, being able to play violin, classical guitar and was now turning her attention to the piano. Annie enjoyed their sessions together, helping Claudine to prepare for an examination she would taking in the New Year.

Claudine attended the local secondary school, but had negotiated with her teachers to have some time out of her school day for the lessons. Most of the time, Claudine had lessons after school, but with the dark evenings drawing in, her parents were happier if she had a lesson earlier in the day. Her father always picked her up in his red sports car, thanking Annie most profusely for the lessons.

As usual, the lesson went very well, although Claudine's mind seemed to be elsewhere some of the time. The hour's lesson went all too quickly, and soon the girl's father was ringing the doorbell. Claudine seemed quite reticent to leave, with her father coaxing her, 'Come on Claudine, time to go home and leave this lady in peace.'

Claudine eventually put her musical notations away, and headed off through the door, followed swiftly by her father. Annie waved them goodbye, noting that she didn't even know Claudine's father's name, having not been formally introduced. There was something about him she didn't like.

Claudine had another lesson two weeks later, and again was preoccupied. Annie almost felt compelled to ask her if everything was okay, but decided against it, as Claudine became more animated as her fingers glided effortlessly along the piano keys. She certainly was talented, Annie thought to herself.

As before, the girl seemed to become more anxious when the doorbell rang, and her father stepped into the hall. Annie decided to make conversation with him whilst Claudine cleared her paperwork away.

'Do you know, I must apologise, but I don't even know your name,' said Annie.

'Oh, it's Nigel.' He proffered his hand, which Annie duly shook. His hand felt icy-cold, and the handshake was limp. Annie recalled something her grandmother Anne had always said, that a limp handshake was a sign of a poor character in a person. Claudine joined her father in the hall, and the final lesson before Christmas was duly arranged. As they went out of the door, Annie observed Nigel putting his hand in the curve of Claudine's back and almost pushing her out.

Something is not quite right there she thought as she closed the door. That evening over dinner, she mentioned the incident to Michael, who much to her chagrin did not seem to be very interested. He was very busy at work, and would frequently come home mentally exhausted, just wanting to relax in front of the TV. Since the start of the autumn term, he had agreed to increase his teaching hours, to help cover for sickness. The effect of the extra hours was taking its toll on him. Normally, Michael was a calm and easy-going person, but lately he had become more snappy and irritable. Annie decided she would have to wait to talk to him about it during his break.

The Christmas holidays arrived, and Annie and Michael were doing some last-minute Christmas shopping. There was a magical atmosphere in a lot of the shops, which Annie loved, although poor Michael was constantly yawning. They decided to stop for coffee, and treated themselves to a festive warm mince pie. Annie was crossing items off her Christmas shopping list as Michael happily munched his mince pie.

'Have we nearly got it all?' he asked, a hopeful look on his face. Annie reassured him, telling him they had only one more shop to visit. Finishing their refreshments, they walked through the busy shopping mall, and Annie spotted Claudine and her father walking swiftly in the opposite direction to them. Again, Annie noticed Nigel's hand in the hollow of Claudine's back. She quietly pointed this out to Michael, but they had gone past by the time he realised what she was saying. Stopping to pretend to look in a shop window, Annie watched the girl and her father disappear around the corner, and suddenly felt compelled to follow them. She told Michael to wait for her, saying she had forgotten something. Michael luckily spotted a vacant seat in the shopping mall, and said to Annie he would wait for her there.

'Okay,' Annie muttered as she walked quickly in the direction of the father and daughter. Turning the corner, she managed to see them ahead, and began following their footsteps, as they wove in and out of the crowd. They did not appear to be looking in any shops, as they were walking quite quickly, as if on a mission. Eventually, they stopped outside a pub, and to Annie's surprise they went inside. She had to make sure they did not see her, so she loitered around the pub entrance, watching them go up to the bar. She noticed that Nigel was directing Claudine to an empty seat by the window, and he then ordered some drinks. He took the drinks over to where Claudine was sitting. Unfortunately, Annie's view was suddenly restricted by a group of young men, who were chatting and standing in her line of vision. She remained there for a few more minutes, but eventually and with reluctance, she decided to return to Michael. She relayed what had happened to her husband, who again was not really interested.

'I think you are getting too involved in all this,' Michael warned, as they returned to the car to drive home. Annie disagreed, and decided she would discuss it with Claudine during her lesson the following week.

Chapter 18

It was getting closer to Christmas, and the weather had decided to turn quite mild, making getting out and about easier for Annie and Michael. Serendipity was looking very festive, with all the rooms adorned with Christmas decorations. Even outside looked good, as they had decided to put some lights around the large oak tree at the front of the house, which added to the ambience. As usual, John and Rose would be visiting, and Lawrence was returning from America, where he had been working. He would be arriving on Christmas Eve, as would Rachel and Liam.

It will be great to have everyone together this Christmas, Annie thought as she wrapped her final present and placed it under the tree. She reflected on the previous Christmas, and her late mother's activities. Although she felt sadness at the loss of Millie, she was relieved to think Christmas would not be so fraught this year.

But before that, Claudine would be coming for her final piano lesson that year. Annie wasn't really looking forward to it, being unsure as to how she was going to broach the subject of Claudine and her father. Reminded of Michael's warning to leave things be, she was tempted to take his advice. However, she changed her mind when Claudine arrived ten minutes late for her lesson, looking quite teary-eyed. It was not like her to be late, and Annie knew there was something wrong when her father had not dropped her off as usual.

'Is everything alright?' she tentatively asked Claudine.

'Everything's fine.' The teenager quickly removed her coat and sat in front of the piano, poised for her lesson, so Annie decided to follow suit. She was going to practise the two tunes that she would be tested on in her forthcoming exam. Claudine began to play the first tune. The sound was captivating. Annie could find no fault with it, and the second was just as good. The lesson was an hour long, but they had completed what Annie wanted to achieve in thirty-five minutes. Annie offered Claudine a drink and a mince pie, which she gratefully accepted. Her whole demeanour had changed once she had begun to play. Annie decided to try and find out why her father hadn't given her a lift.

'Oh, he's busy today, so I had to get the bus,' said Claudine, avoiding eye contact.

Tenacious by nature, Annie wasn't going to give up. 'So he won't be picking you up today?'

'No.'

'I see.' Annie cleared her throat and said, 'I noticed you seemed a bit upset when you arrived earlier.'

'Did I?' Claudine looked at her quizzically.

Annie could see that Claudine wasn't going to open up easily. As they sipped their tea in companionable silence, Annie contemplated her next approach. She was no expert at this sort of thing, but she had grown very fond of Claudine over the time in which she had been having lessons, and was genuinely concerned for her well-being. Eventually, she said, 'How is your Christmas shopping going?'

'Okay, thanks. I have nearly got all my presents.'

'Do you have a lot of people to buy for?'

'Not really, my mum and my stepdad, and a few friends from school – oh, and my aunty Jane.'

'So Nigel is your stepdad?' Annie felt a bit like she was prying, but she was curious.

'Yes. My real dad left when I was only five. Mum and I were on our own for several years, until Mum met Nigel.'

'It must have been difficult for you to get used to having another dad.' Annie noticed Claudine seemed to physically tense up following this statement.

'Not really. Nigel is very good to Mum.'

'What about you?' Annie saw this as an opportunity to find out more.

Claudine avoided Annie's gaze and, looking downwards, said quietly, 'He's good to me as well.'

'Is he? In what way is he good to you?'

Claudine began to twitch nervously, playing with her cardigan sleeve. She didn't answer straight away, and finally said, 'I think I'd better be going now, I've taken up enough of your time. We've certainly gone beyond the hour's lesson.'

Annie felt deflated, and knew the moment was lost. 'That's okay. I enjoy your company. It's nice to chat about other things, apart from music and your exam.'

Claudine got up to go, picking up her coat.

'Have you got far to go? I can drop you off if you like,' Annie offered.

'Oh, I don't want to put you to any trouble.'

'It's no trouble, honestly. It's getting dark outside. Anyway, where did you catch the bus from on the way here?' Claudine didn't seem to know the answer to Annie's last question, and became quite flustered. Annie continued, 'I know there aren't many buses that come out this way. Perhaps I could drop you at the bus stop, if you won't let me drive you home.'

Claudine began to collect up her things in preparation to go. 'I'm not sure where the bus stop back is, but I'm sure I shall find it,' she said as she strode towards the front door.

Annie was determined to stop her. 'Look, I'll drive you home. You can give me directions, or I can use my satnav in the car.'

Eventually, Claudine did concede, and Annie took her home. It was quite a distance from Serendipity. The satnav said 12.5 miles. The house was set in a cul-de-sac of detached houses. Annie could see the lights on in the house, but there was no sign of Nigel's red sports car. The conversation in the car had reverted to music, so she was unable to explore Claudine's situation any further. Claudine thanked her most profusely for the lift, and wished her a merry Christmas.

'You, too. I will see you at the next lesson – 10th of January I believe. If you need a lift, let me know, won't you?'

'Thanks, but I should be able to have a lift.'

Annie waved as she drove out of the cul-de-sac, leaving Claudine standing on the pavement. On the journey home, she ruminated over how the hell she was going to get the truth out of her.

The time seemed to fly past, and before they knew it, the day before Christmas Eve had arrived. Rose and John were due later that evening. Annie was busy tidying the house, and preparing the rooms for her guests. She felt a buzz of excitement at the thought of seeing her favourite son and daughter-in-law. As they sat and watched TV, Annie received a text message from Rose, saying they would be late, as they were stuck in a traffic jam. She conveyed this information to Michael, but it fell on deaf ears as he had fallen asleep.

Eventually, Rose and John arrived at 10.30pm, feeling fraught and tired. There had been an accident on the motorway, which had caused traffic chaos.

'Never mind, you're here now, safe and sound,' said Annie as she took their coats and Michael transported their luggage to their room. She made drinks, and soon the conversation was flowing nicely. However, before long, John was yawning frequently, and a suggestion was made for all to retire to bed, after a nightcap.

Annie remained downstairs, and decided to have a second nightcap. She wasn't feeling particularly tired, and was still reflecting on the Claudine dilemma. She decided to discuss it with Rose the next day, as Michael had been no help.

Lawrence arrived around 10.30 on Christmas Eve morning. He was his usual quiet self, not giving much away about his time in New York. He had been over there as part of a medical research team, looking into something to do with diabetes. This was all the information Annie had, as Lawrence was not forthcoming on any of the details. Although, later in the day he seemed to chat more freely about the study to Rose, whose shared medical knowledge meant she would understand the terms he was using.

Rachel and Liam appeared at 5pm, and all were seated around the dining room table at 6pm. Annie had prepared a Christmas Eve supper for all to enjoy. As they tucked into cold roast chicken and salad with buttered new potatoes, the conversation flowed freely. Rachel was in her last year at university, and had a lot of work to do for her psychology degree over the festive season. Liam teased her, saying he had no work to do as his university days were over.

'Well, you can help me with mine!' Rachel demanded, grabbing his hand playfully. The meal ended with drinks all round, and lots of cheering going on. The evening carried on in much the same vein. There was no mention of Millie, or last year's escapades. Eventually, everyone except Annie and Rose decided to retire to bed.

Rose smiled at Annie. 'The meal was delicious, especially the afters!' The afters being apple pie and custard.

'I'm glad you enjoyed it.'

As they sipped their Baileys, curled up comfortably in armchairs in the lounge, the conversation turned to Millie. Annie expressed her feelings to Rose, saying how she missed her mother terribly, but was looking forward to a more peaceful Christmas this year.

'I'm sure you are. You deserve a quieter time this year,' said Rose.

Annie decided now was the time to share her fears about Claudine with Rose, who listened attentively whilst Annie told the tale. She then sought Rose's opinion as to what she should do next.

'It's a really difficult subject to discuss with anyone who you think is being abused. A friend of mine's daughter had a friend who was being abused and it took some time for it to come out in the open. But once it was discovered, the girl was thankful she'd had the courage to reveal the abuse. It was her uncle who was doing the abusing and he was interviewed by the police, and it came to light that he had been abusing other young girls, too. I believe he is now serving a sentence in prison.'

'So do you think I should encourage Claudine to speak out, or just keep out of it?' Annie asked as she sipped her Baileys, enjoying the warm feeling it gave as it slipped down her throat.

'Do you think she would open up to you?'

'I'm not sure, really. We do get on very well, but it is such a delicate subject to discuss.'

'Why don't you see how she is at her next lesson, and take it from there?' Rose suggested, downing the last drop of Baileys.

'Yes, that's a good idea.'

They clinked their empty glasses together and decided to go off to bed. Tomorrow was Christmas Day, and there were meals to cook, presents to open, and plenty of good cheer to enjoy!

Chapter 19

Christmas day dawned with a clear bright blue sky, dotted with the occasional fluffy cloud. There was a definite nip in the air when Annie ventured out to feed the birds. As she prepared the vegetables for lunch, she reflected on the past year. There had been moments of sadness, with Millie's death, but also happy times, with Rose and John's wedding.

I suppose that's what life is all about with its ups and downs, Annie concluded. She recalled that her grandmother Anne would call them the "trials and tribulations of life".

Annie was deep in her own thoughts, and didn't hear Rose enter the kitchen. They wished each other a happy Christmas, and Rose offered to help.

'Have some tea first,' said Annie, pouring out a cup for Rose. 'I seem to remember you helped me last year, too!'

'I don't mind. It's not fair that you should be doing it all anyway,' said Rose as she sipped her tea.

'It's nice to have some company, but I enjoy cooking, and it's great to get the appreciative nods from all the family.'

They settled into a companionable silence, and slowly everyone began to appear in the kitchen, and Christmas wishes were exchanged. Once the food preparations were complete, it was time to open presents. Following the usual ritual of one person at a time opening a present, the morning passed with much frivolity, interspersed with many a thank you being offered as each person admired their presents.

Christmas lunch followed, and everyone sat in their usual seats, with Annie and Michael at either end of the long mahogany table. Christmas carols were playing softly in the background while everyone chatted and made approving sounds as they consumed their food. Annie cast her eye over the table, marvelling in the delight of having all her family around her. Lawrence intent on eating his food as quickly as he could. Rachel eating at a slower pace, and frequently casting loving glances at Liam, who was smiling back. Rose and John just simply eating and chatting about amusing incidents in their respective jobs and Michael giving her one of his appreciative smiles.

After lunch, everyone retired to the lounge to prepare to watch the mandatory Queen's speech on TV at 3pm. Much had happened over the year, both politically and economically, with the unprecedented crash of all the banks and building societies, and the constant threat from terrorists. Annie always thought that the Queen was able to put a different perspective on it all, emphasising the importance of Christianity and family values.

After the speech, some of them decided to go out for a walk. It was still very cold, but the sky had remained a bright cerulean blue, although the sunlight was beginning to fade as the afternoon moved on. Donning their coats, scarves and gloves, Annie, Michael, Rose and John ventured out.

'We'll leave you young ones to lounge around while we get our exercise!' shouted Michael, as they all piled out of the front door. Receiving no response from Rachel, Liam or Lawrence, he deduced that they had probably not heard his facetious comment.

They walked in a comfortable silence along the main road, taking in the wonderful scenery around them. Annie was so glad they lived in a rural spot, and conveyed this sentiment to the rest of the group.

'Yes, it's lovely around here,' said Rose, pulling her scarf up around her neck. As the sun began to sink and the temperature was falling, they walked briskly for about a mile, and then decided to turn back and return to Serendipity.

They appreciated the warmth exuding from the hallway as they entered the house. Annie was soon making tea, and slices of Christmas cake were offered round. The evening passed uneventfully, with everyone suitably satiated.

Gradually, all retired to bed, leaving Annie and Michael in the lounge. Michael reached for Annie's hand and said, 'It's been a lovely day, sharing it with all the family, the superb lunch and all my great presents.' He kissed her on the mouth and spontaneously, Annie returned the kiss with a passion, and before long they were in each other's arms, and rolling on the floor like a pair of teenagers.

Annie began to giggle as Michael gently bit her ear and then whispered softly, 'I think we should go to bed, what do you think?'

'Oh, I agree,' chuckled Annie, and Michael grabbed her hand, helping her up, and the two made their way upstairs as quickly as they could while their ardour was still rising.

On Boxing Day, they all spent another relaxing day together, which involved eating, drinking, chatting, watching TV, and generally chilling out. Annie managed to chat with Lawrence for a short time, and found out that he had actually met someone whilst in New York and that the pair were frequently corresponding by text, Skype, and planned to meet up in the new year. The lady in question was called Bianca, and she worked as a doctor at the hospital where Lawrence had been doing his research. She was from New York, but her parents originated from Mexico.

'Do you have a picture of Bianca, by any chance?' Annie tentatively asked.

'Yes, I have one on my phone,' said Lawrence who began searching his phone, for a photo. Eventually, he found one and showed it to Annie. The picture was of a dark-haired, pretty girl, with deep brown eyes, tanned skin, and a captivating smile.

'She looks lovely,' said Annie, noticing a blush developing on Lawrence's face. He smiled at her and said, 'She is a very nice person, and a good doctor too.'

'How old is she?'

'She's twenty-nine, a bit older than me.'

'That's okay,' said Annie wondering why this was important. Their conversation was interrupted by Michael, who announced a request for tea and Christmas cake or mince pies.

'Who wants what?' asked Annie, and requests were duly made, and she roped Lawrence in to helping her. She was glad that at last she had managed to find something out about her reserved son and his love life.

The remainder of the week leading up to the New Year passed in much the same relaxing vein. Rachel and Liam decided to visit the shops, as they had some gift vouchers to spend, and Lawrence went with them. They all went for lunch at the local pub one day, and tried to get out for daily walks, to burn off all those extra calories. The weather remained cold but dry, so all were grateful for this.

Early on New Year's Eve, Annie was out in the garden as usual, feeding the birds. The morning was frosty but dry, the sky a bright azure blue, so she decided to go through the secret gate. All the family were still in bed, so she wouldn't be missed. She noted that the gate was getting very creaky as she wedged it open, realising that she hadn't been through it for a few months. Once through the gate, the view of the open countryside never failed to thrill Annie. She soon found herself walking through the frost-laden grass, towards the trees and the brook. She stood under the shadow of the bare trees and listened to the sound of the babbling water, and instinctively began to chat to Anne, and then Millie, telling them about how she was enjoying Christmas with all the family, but how she missed them both, and hoped they were happy wherever they were. She could hear a bird chirping in the trees, then a robin appeared and perched itself very close to her. She watched it as it bobbed along, and wondered if it had been sent by Anne or Millie.

What a lot of nonsense! she told herself, but secretly hoped that it was true. She made her way back towards the house, and then through the secret gate. She could hear her name being called, so she moved quickly towards the back door, where she found Michael staring at her quizzically.

'Where have you been? I have been calling you for the last five minutes!'

'Oh, I was just in the orchard... counting the number of trees. Some of them don't look very healthy.' Michael gave her another quizzical look, as if he didn't really believe her. She was rescued by Rose and John, who had entered the kitchen, looking for breakfast.

Food preparations begin once again! Annie thought to herself as she put the kettle on.

Eventually, night-time came, and as the clock struck midnight to welcome in 2009, they were all gathered in the front garden, enjoying the firework display overhead. They didn't linger for long once the fireworks had finished, as it was very cold. The weatherman had forecast some snow later in the day. Once inside, there were drinks all round, and clinking of glasses as they all wished each other a happy New Year. Annie was asked to play the customary *Silent Worship*, which was followed by a fervent applause and much merriment. Unfortunately, John didn't accompany her on his electric guitar, although there were some who were relieved he didn't join in, including Rose.

The rest of New Year's Day passed quietly, with most people feeling tired after the late night. Annie, Rose, John and Michael went for a walk, and ended up at the local pub. They sat drinking their various tipples beside a comforting log fire, and went on to discuss Rachel, Liam and Lawrence.

'Lawrence has always been quite secretive about his love life,' said Annie.

'I don't blame him, with you jumping to conclusions about this girl he has met in New York.'

'What do you mean?'

'Well, he has only just met her, and you've got them married off already!'

'I have not!' Annie retorted.

'Hey, you two, I'm sure Lawrence will let us know if anything develops between him and this girl,' John interjected. Both his parents gave him a look which said *stop interfering with our discussions*. However, they moved on to discuss Rachel and Liam, and concluded that nothing much would be happening there until Rachel had finished her degree.

Soon Lawrence, Rachel and Liam were packing up to return to their respective homes. Rose and John would be staying a bit longer. The snow had fallen, but had just been flurries, so nothing to cause any travel problems. The thin blanket of snow created a really festive feel as they all trotted out for their daily walk. John and Michael walked on ahead, leaving Rose and Annie behind, deep in conversation. The issue of Claudine was the topic, and Rose enquired whether Annie was going to explore it further.

'Like you said, I'll have to see how she is when she comes for her lesson on the tenth of this month.'

'Yes, I think that's the best way to tackle it. I mean, you may have got it all wrong.'

'That's what Michael says. He thinks I should keep out of it.'

'He may be right. Just see how it goes. If you want to chat about it afterwards, give me a ring, won't you,' said Rose, linking arms with Annie as they continued their walk. Annie always felt better after talking to Rose; she had such a reassuring manner about her, which must be very useful in her nursing role, Annie thought.

The day came for Rose and John to leave, and after many goodbyes, the pair drove off, leaving Annie and Michael waving on the doorstep.

'Well, that's Christmas and New Year over for another year,' said Michael as he grasped Annie's hand.

'Yes, I wonder what 2009 will bring?'

'I wonder!' said Michael, as they closed the front door and went into the warm, cosy lounge.

So much had happened at Serendipity over the decades. The grand old house had seen three generations of the same family, all with their own stories to tell. Who knew what the future might hold for those to come? The house would stay the same, but the inhabitants would always change over time.

.

www.ingramcontent.com/pod-product-compliance
Lightning Source LLC
Chambersburg PA
CBHW030304100526
44590CB00012B/517